PHILOSOPHY

A BEGINNER'S GUIDE TO THE IDEAS OF
100 GREAT THINKERS

PHILOSOPHY

A BEGINNER'S GUIDE TO THE IDEAS OF
100 GREAT THINKERS

JEREMY HARWOOD

Quercus

Contents

THE POST-MODERN ERA 143

What is philosophy?

'Philosophy,' the great Greek philosopher Plato wrote, 'begins in wonder.' Since his time, countless thinkers have tried to pin down exactly what philosophy is. Put at its simplest, it is the quest for enlightenment that began when human beings first started to try to comprehend the world through the power of reason. It is a questioning that seeks to probe into the most fundamental aspects of human existence. It also asks questions about the nature of human perception, experience, knowledge and understanding.

Traditionally, philosophy is split into a number of branches. There is metaphysics, which inquires into the nature of reality; ontology, which is concerned specifically with studying the nature of being; logic, which, as its name implies, sets out the principles for valid reasoning; epistemology, which investigates the nature of knowledge; and ethics, which can be defined broadly as the study of morality. In addition, philosophy has spread its wings to concern itself with other vital areas of human activity, including language, politics, art, science, law, religion and, finally, the mind itself.

Schools of thought

Given such broad parameters, it is hardly surprising that there are many different schools of philosophical thought. Indeed, disagreements in philosophy often centre on differences between such schools, which is why knowledge of what they teach is important in developing understanding of the cut and thrust of philosophical debate.

Historically, there were the sceptics, who doubted whether it was possible to know anything at all for certain; the empiricists, who claimed that all knowledge was based on external experience; the idealists, who postulated that nothing can exist independently of human thought; and the utilitarians, who related basic moral principles, such as concepts of right and wrong, to what makes people happy or unhappy.

In more recent times there have been the logical positivists, who sought to clarify the meanings of concepts and ideas, and the existentialists, including Jean-Paul Sartre,

the school's founding father. Finally, there are the analytical philosophers, such as Bertrand Russell and Ludwig Wittgenstein, whose analysis of the roots of language had such a profound effect on subsequent philosophical developments in the English-speaking world.

Philosophers differ

There have been many others – there are probably as many different points of view as there are philosophers. Some, like St Augustine and St Thomas Aquinas, put their faith in a higher power. Others, including Leibniz, have been optimists, while the likes of Hobbes have taken a darker and more pessimistic view of the human condition. Many, such as Hegel and, most notably, Nietzsche, have been misunderstood and, in Nietzsche's case in particular, had what they wrote distorted by others to serve their own purposes. Marx, for one, claimed infallibility, while others have refused to try to provide any concrete answers at all.

In this book you will be able to examine the speculations of the most influential philosophers and assess the significance – and the validity – of their often divergent philosophical views. You will also discover that, despite their differences, the great thinkers of yesterday, today and even tomorrow all had, have or will have the same goal in mind: to push back the boundaries of human knowledge and understanding and to bring to light what has hitherto been hidden from the human mind.

The Ancient World

The origins of philosophy lie in our need to understand the world we live in.
Around the sixth century BC, in the West, early Greek philosophers began to
question fundamentals that had to that time largely been taken for granted.
In India, Siddhartha Gautama – the Buddha – was embarking on his quest
for enlightenment, while in China, Confucius and Lao-tzu were laying the
foundations of two contrasting schools of thought – Confucianism and Taoism.

Early Greek thinkers tried to understand the world through logic and reason.
By the time of Socrates, Plato and Aristotle, Greek philosophers started
speculating about how people should conduct their lives.

In India, the Buddha focused on the practicalities of human existence.
By following his precepts, he asserted it was possible to achieve a state of
ultimate happiness. In China, Confucius asserted the values of filial piety,
respect for tradition and the close observance of moral order in his teachings.
Lao-tzu was more individualistic in his thinking, believing that following the
path to enlightenment should be the ultimate goal.

Thales of Melitus

c.620 BC−c.540 BC

Generally accepted as being the first analytic philosopher and natural scientist to emerge in Western intellectual history, Thales is renowned for the way in which he tried to find a rational explanation for the underlying nature of all things in the natural world.

A wealthy philosopher

Perhaps the most renowned of all the so-called pre-Socratic philosophers – and the first of the Seven Sages of classical Greek tradition – Thales was a multi-faceted man with a wide range of interests. As well as being the founder of analytical philosophy, he was a noted astronomer, geographer, mathematician and engineer; he was also a shrewd businessman who made a fortune out of olives.

Analytical philosophy

Thales was the first to propose explanations of natural phenomena that were based on reason rather than on theology or mythology,

ABOVE: **The early thinker Thales believed that the world was made of a single element. He mistakenly thought that this was water.**

and the question that most preoccupied him was what the world is made of. He concluded that it must all consist of one single element – water. The earth floated on an underlying sea, and earthquakes occurred when the earth was rocked by subterranean waves. Realizing that water could turn into vapour when it evaporated, become solid through freezing and that all life needed it in order to exist, he deduced that it must be the fundamental building block of the natural world.

Anaximander

*c.*610 BC*–c.*546 BC

The first thinker to develop a systematic philosophical view of the world, Anaximander argued that the essence of all things was not a substance but something he called the apeiron, *a boundless, inexhaustible creative source extending limitlessly in all directions.*

Thales's heir

A geographer, geometer, biologist and astronomer as well as a philosopher, Anaximander, one of the most important pre-Socratic philosophers, took over Thales's school. However, he disputed Thales's claim that water was the fundamental element, postulating that, together with air, earth and fire, it was one of the four elements that shaped the earth and everything that lived upon it.

Apeiron

Claiming that nature is ruled by laws, Anaximander held that the universe was boundless and the number of worlds in it infinite. So,

ABOVE: **Anaximander is the first known philosopher to have written down his studies, although only a fragment remains.**

too, was the *apeiron*, the all-powerful primary source, the originator of everything that he and his fellow thinkers had been seeking.

Anaximander also disputed Thales's assertion that the earth was supported by the sea, as the sea would have to be supported by something else and so on ad infinitum. He came up with the revolutionary hypothesis that the earth was a solid object, probably a cylindrical drum, hanging in space. His speculations concerning *apeiron* and the physical nature of the earth and the heavens advanced philosophical thought considerably.

BIOGRAPHY

Name Anaximander

Born c.610 BC

Place Melitus, Asia Minor

Nationality Greek

Key facts His philosophical speculations and those concerning the nature of the universe make him one of history's greatest philosophers. He drew a revolutionary map of the heavens and the first known map of the world.

Died c.546 BC

KEY WORKS

• *On Nature* (fragment)

Siddhartha Gautama

THE BUDDHA *c.560 BC—c.480 BC*

As much a religious leader as a philosopher, the Buddha is said to have found enlightenment at the age of 35 while meditating beneath a fig tree. He spent the rest of his life encouraging others to embark on the quest to find nirvana, a state of ultimate insight and bliss, and escape from human suffering.

BIOGRAPHY

Name Siddhartha Gautama

Born c.560 BC

Place Lumbini, modern Nepal

Nationality Indian

Key facts Ending the cycle of birth and rebirth and achieving nirvana is the essence of the Buddha's teaching. His philosophy laid the foundations for a whole new way of thinking that today has a global following.

Died c.480 BC

KEY WORKS

• *Sutra Pitaka*

The man and his teachings

The son of a minor provincial ruler, the Buddha left his home in northern India at the age of 29 at the start of his long search for enlightenment. His teachings originally took root in southern Asia, spreading from there throughout the Asiatic continent and, in more recent times, the world.

The Buddha was a pragmatist. He dismissed attempts to answer abstract philosophical questions, such as those relating to the nature of the universe, considering them unanswerable. Instead, he focused on the practical, which was why he urged the necessity of assessing and testing his precepts against personal experience rather than simply accepting them without question. Only by finding a middle way between the extremes of dogmatism and scepticism would people be able to take the first steps towards enlightenment and truth.

According to the Buddha, life revolves around a perpetual cycle of birth and rebirth and is dominated by suffering. Wealth, social position, power, sensual pleasures and even meditation are all impermanent and lead to dissatisfaction. None can generate the lasting happiness to which humanity should aspire. That, the Buddha believed, can be achieved only by following a clearly defined spiritual path, involving special ethical and mental training. It involved awareness of the fundamental moral law of the universe, karma, which states that good actions produce good consequences and bad actions bad ones.

The Buddha's works

The Buddha did not write anything down. His teachings were passed on orally for three centuries, and the earliest collection of Buddhist texts, the most important being the *Sutra Pitaka* (a series of dialogues between the Buddha, his disciples and other contemporaries), was probably compiled in Sri Lanka some time during the first century BC.

The Noble Truths

The Buddha summed up his doctrines in what he termed the Four Noble Truths. The first makes it clear that unenlightened human existence inevitably involves suffering, and the second explains what causes this condition and how reflection, meditation and direct experience all combine in helping to understand it. The third truth explains that it is possible to break free from this treadmill by ceasing to crave or want and by renouncing everything that generates suffering for individuals and for others. The fourth sets out how this can be achieved by following the Noble Eightfold Path, the Buddha's route map to ultimate enlightenment, involving training in wisdom, ethics, right-mindedness and concentration.

The Buddha's teachings – that in order to reach true peace one must break the cycle through enlightenment – had a tremendous impact throughout Asia. They are also mirrored in the thinking of several prominent Western philosophers, notably Immanuel Kant, Arthur Schopenhauer and, to a lesser extent, David Hume.

13

Confucius

c.551 BC—c.479 BC

China's most influential thinker, whose aim was to restore the moral integrity of society and the state, Confucius, or K'ung Fu-Tzu, put forward many practical precepts to show how his ideal of a harmonious, stable social order could be achieved.

The man

Much of what is known about Confucius and his life is legend. What Sima Qian, the official court historian of the Han dynasty, tells us is that he endured a poverty-stricken childhood and, upon reaching manhood, was forced to take a variety of petty, intellectually undemanding jobs. It was not until he reached the age of 50 that his talents were finally recognized and he was appointed first Minister of Public Works and subsequently Minister of Justice by the ruling duke of the region. Soon, however, Confucius apparently fell out with influential members of the local nobility and was forced into exile. Eventually, in around 484 BC, he returned, spending the rest of his life teaching. He never aspired to high office again.

Analects

The best source for developing an understanding of Confucius and his thought is the *Analects*, the work on which much of his reputation rests. It is problematic, however, as it was compiled, it seems, long after the great sage's death – and then not even by his direct disciples, but by disciples of those disciples. Consequently, some of its texts are inconsistent and incompatible with Confucian thought.

LEFT: **Confucius taught that filial piety and respect for tradition were essential elements in formulating the ethics which people should always observe.**

> ❝ *To be able under all circumstances to practise five things constitutes perfect virtue; these five things are gravity, generosity of soul, sincerity, earnestness and kindness.* ❞

Ren, the Golden Rule and *Li*

Confucius's thinking is bound up with the concept of what he termed *Ren*, compassion for others. To cultivate this he urged his disciples to observe the ethical precepts encapsulated in his Golden Rule: 'Never impose on others what you would not choose for yourself.'

Confucius explained that people needed to learn the importance of self-restraint. They also needed to master the principles of *Li* (ritual forms of behaviour and respect), regardless of individual rank and station. Just as children have certain duties to their parents, he said, so rulers have duties to their subjects. Reconciling personal desires with the needs of other members of one's family and the community is one step along the road to establishing a harmonious, stable society for the benefit of all.

Moral order and example

For Confucius, moral order – in the family, the state and in the world – should be the ultimate goal. Achieving it depended primarily on undertaking long, careful study. No one, he said, could achieve this overnight. He used his own life as an example. In the *Analects*, he states: 'From the age of 15, I have been intent on learning; from 30, I have established myself; from 40, I have not been confused; from 50, I have known the mandate of Heaven; from 60, my ear has been attuned; from 70, I have followed my heart's desire without transgressing what is right.'

Politically, his philosophy is rooted in the belief that leaders at all levels of society should lead by moral example. A ruler who discharges his duties conscientiously is much more likely to command the loyalty of his subjects. They, in turn, will be more likely to willingly fulfil their allocated social roles.

The goal of human society was to achieve the kind of moral order that he said existed in *Tian* (Heaven).

BIOGRAPHY

Name K'ung Fu-Tzu

Born c.551 BC

Place Qufu, China

Nationality Chinese

Key facts Preaching the virtues of wisdom, self-knowledge, courage and understanding, Confucius argued that the pursuit of virtue should be the universal goal, with *Jen* (benevolence) the most important moral quality that anyone can possess.

Died c.479 BC

KEY WORKS

• *Analects*

Heraclitus

*c.*600 BC–*c.*540 BC

Best known for his beliefs that all things exist in a state of flux, opposites coincide and that fire is the core element out of which the world is made, Heraclitus argued that, although the universe is eternal, it is in a constant state of change.

BIOGRAPHY

Name Heraclitus

Born c.600 BC

Place Ephesus, Asia Minor

Nationality Greek

Key facts He believed that fire was the primary element and that it had its counterpart in the human soul. He argued that the constant strife between opposites was the driving force ensuring that everything existed in a state of flux.

Died c.540 BC

KEY WORKS

• No known written works

Flux

Heraclitus asserted that permanence in the universe does not exist, the only constant being change. He does not explain his thinking in any great detail, however, and the fragments of his teaching that survive in others' works are often obscure.

The unity of opposites

He stated that the three principle elements were fire, earth and water. Fire was the primary element, controlling and modifying the other two. The dynamism existing between opposites provides the universe with its driving force – the unity of opposites. Everything depends on opposing tendencies coming together and the tension between them, causing the universe to exist in a state of flux.

Heraclitus used the analogy of a river to explain his point. Although the waters are constantly moving the river stays the same. Indeed, it is precisely because there are rivers at all that the waters are constantly moving. Although the universe itself is eternal, nothing remains changeless within it because of the transformation of fire.

RIGHT: **Heraclitus, also known as the 'weeping philosopher', proposed that change was the only constant in the universe.**

Parmenides

c. 510 BC — c. 450 BC

One of the most important of all the pre-Socratic philosophers by virtue of being the first to use deductive reasoning, Parmenides believed that appearances were all deceptive, change impossible and that reality is singular, undivided and homogenous.

On Nature

Few details are known about Parmenides's life. He was a pupil of Xenophanes – another notable pre-Socratic philosopher – came from a noble family and played a role in the governance of Elea, a Greek colony in Italy. All that survives of his work – enough to give an insight into his thinking – are 150 lines (out of an estimated total of 3,000) of *On Nature*, a long poem in which he described an encounter with a goddess and the revelation he received.

'One cannot know that which is not, nor utter it'

He claimed that it is impossible to talk or think about something that

does not exist, so it follows that anything that can be thought and spoken of must exist, even if only in the mind. It followed that to think of anything that *is* logically implies the existence of something that *is not*. Nothing can come into existence; nothing can be destroyed. Both are illusory, as are movement, change and plurality.

He is important because he made the first known attempt at logical deduction and probed into such enduring major philosophical problems as the nature of existence and the relationship between thought, language and reality.

BIOGRAPHY

Name Parmenides

Born c.510 BC

Place Elea, Italy

Nationality Greek

Key facts He is noted as being the first thinker to employ deductive reasoning to justify his claim that anything that can be thought and spoken of, by definition, must exist.

Died c.450 BC

KEY WORKS

• *On Nature* (fragment)

LEFT: **Parmenides' speculations on perception and reality made him one of the most significant pre-Socratic thinkers.**

Lao-tzu

c.6TH CENTURY BC

Whether or not this Chinese philosopher actually lived is a matter of debate, and the thoughts attributed to him may in fact be the work of a later individual or group. His importance derives from his supposed authorship of the Tao Te Ch'ing (The Way and Its Power), *the core text of Taoism.*

BIOGRAPHY

Name Lao-tzu (Old Master)

Born c.6th century BC

Place Ch'u, China

Nationality Chinese

Key facts Although it is unclear who Lao-tzu was – or even if he existed – we do know that the *Tao Te Ch'ing*, the book attached to his name, is the most important work in Taoist philosophy.

Died c.5th or 6th century BC

KEY WORKS

• *Tao Te Ch'ing*

The Tao Te Ch'ing

Some believe that there was a real Lao-tzu and that he was a slightly older contemporary of Confucius. According to Sima Qian, the court historian of the Han dynasty, he certainly did exist, working for 50 years in the Chinese emperor's library and gradually becoming known as a mystic for his deep wisdom. Eventually, he decided to abandon the emperor, perhaps to escape what he saw as the moral decay of city life or possibly because his fellow men were unwilling to follow the path to natural goodness. He headed towards the mountains and Tibet, and when he approached the gate in the wall that marked the empire's boundary, the gatekeeper asked him to compile a written record of his wisdom. The *Tao Te Ch'ing* was the result.

Some still accept this account as broadly accurate; others argue that Lao-tzu was a legendary figure and the *Tao Te Ch'ing* a compilation of philosophical precepts by several Taoist scholars who adopted the pen-name of Lao-tzu.

Taoism and its principles

Whatever the truth, it is indisputable that, together with Confucianism, Taoism is a distinct philosophical response to the problems its author – or authors – saw confronting Chinese society at the time the *Tao Te Ch'ing* was written.

Taoism offers a very different solution from Confucianism. Where Confucianism is a pragmatic, practical philosophy, Taoism is based on mysticism. The nature of the *Tao* itself is obscure. Literally, the word means 'way' or 'path', but the *Tao Te Ch'ing* makes it clear that it is the name for something that, by definition, cannot be named or fully grasped. However, it can be followed. The *Tao Te Ch'ing* counsels people to turn away from the folly of human pursuits. Rather than battle against the natural order of things, they should go with the flow.

A true Taoist is ready to renounce materialism, to seek to understand the laws of nature, to work towards developing one's intuitive inner self and, above all, be prepared to lead a peaceful, virtuous life. Searching and striving for anything is basically counter-productive. Far better, the *Tao Te Ch'ing* says, to employ the principles of *wu-wie* – that is, to do nothing. The precept, however, is not to be taken literally. Rather, it is a way of mastering circumstances by understanding their nature and then shaping consequent actions in accordance with them. 'The *Tao*,' the *Tao Te Ch'ing* says, 'abides in non-action. Yet nothing is left undone.'

It is impossible to underestimate the impact of Taoism. It is still influential in Chinese art, literature, religion, politics and philosophy in all its rich complexity.

ABOVE: **Lao-tzu is an important figure in Taoism, whose followers view him as both a wise man and a god.**

Zeno of Elea

*c.*490 BC—*c.*425 BC

Zeno was the first philosopher to write down his thoughts in prose as opposed to verse. His fascinating paradoxes — the best known of which is probably 'Achilles and the Tortoise' — were devised to show that any kind of motion is impossible and that reality is unitary and unchanging.

BIOGRAPHY

Name Zeno

Born *c.*490 BC

Place Elea, Italy

Nationality Greek

Key facts A friend and student of Parmenides, Zeno is best known for the paradoxes he devised. In them he argued that time and space are infinitely divisible and so became the first thinker to demonstrate that the concept of infinity is problematic.

Died *c.*425 BC

KEY WORKS

• The paradoxes (preserved in the works of others)

Zeno's influence

Zeno's influence on the development of Western philosophy is profound. In the 19th century the German philosopher Georg Friedrich Wilhelm von Hegel claimed that Zeno's paradoxes supported his own belief that reality is contradictory; later, the British philosopher Bertrand Russell stated that Zeno's arguments had been the basis for almost all theories of space and time and infinity. According to Aristotle, Zeno was the first thinker in history to pioneer the use of dialectic in argument. Whether he was or not is uncertain, but what is unquestionably true is that his celebrated paradoxes — all of his work that survives, albeit in fragmentary form — display the first known use of the logical technique known as *reductio ad absurdum*, literally 'reduced to absurdity'.

The paradoxes

According to Plato, the paradoxes were devised to defend his master Parmenides's philosophy. Although only nine are now known — having been paraphrased by Aristotle, Plato, Proclus and Simplicius — there are thought to have been 40 of them in all, possibly originally written down. As well as the celebrated 'Achilles and the Tortoise', they include 'The Runner and the Racetrack' and 'The Arrow and the Moving Rows'.

In any paradox, its proponent puts forward an argument that, although it appears sound and seemingly based on logical premises, nevertheless leads to a conclusion that anyone else feels sure must be false. Zeno was the master of this art. Confronted with one of his paradoxes, there are only three possible courses of action: we can reject one or more of his premises, question the logic he employs or accept the paradoxical conclusion. It is a dilemma that is practically impossible to resolve.

'Achilles and the Tortoise'

This paradox, which Zeno devised to demonstrate the illusory nature of motion, is probably the most celebrated example of his particular brand of thinking. Achilles and a tortoise decide to have a race, but, because he can run twice as fast, Achilles agrees to give the tortoise a head start. The race begins. Now, postulates Zeno, by the time Achilles gets to the tortoise's starting point it will have moved ahead by half the distance of its lead. By the time Achilles reaches that point it will have moved on again by half the distance. In other words, Achilles can never catch up with the tortoise no matter how fast he runs because every time he moves the tortoise moves as well.

It is an impeccably logical argument, even though its conclusion is patently false. That was exactly the point Zeno was trying to make. Although various thinkers – notably David Hume, Immanuel Kant and Hegel – devised solutions, none of these is totally successful. Despite this, although there must be a fault in Zeno's logic somewhere, no one has been able to demonstrate conclusively what it is.

LEFT: **Zeno, a pupil of Parmenides, was particularly noted for his celebrated paradoxes, in which a seemingly logical argument leads inevitably to a false conclusion. Some still have not been satisfactorily solved.**

21

Socrates

c.470 BC–c.399 BC

Socrates was the founding father of moral philosophy. It is impossible to underestimate the importance of his impact on subsequent developments in Western philosophical thought.

BIOGRAPHY

Name Socrates

Born c.470 BC

Place Athens

Nationality Greek

Key facts As far as is known, he wrote no works of his own, but taught by means of public discussion and debate. His unconventional views angered the city's authorities so much that they put him on trial, sentencing him to death.

Died c.399 BC

KEY WORKS

• Fragments surviving in Plato's *Apology*, *Crito* and *Phaedo*

Breaking with tradition

Believed to have been the son of a midwife and a stonemason, Socrates became Athens's leading philosopher at a time of great upheaval for the city he loved. What makes him a key figure in the story of Western philosophy is the way in which he broke with the concerns of his contemporaries and of the philosophers of the past. Unlike them, he was simply not concerned about the answers to abstract metaphysical speculations about the nature of the universe, what the world consisted of and how it had been made. He believed that the philosopher's task was much more practical: it was to teach people how they ought to live and show them what a good life might be.

The Socratic method

The way in which Socrates conducted his philosophical inquiries was novel too. He seems not to have had any doctrines or dogmas of his own, nor did he see himself as a teacher, at least in the accepted sense. 'The only thing I know is that I know nothing,' he is reported as saying. The Socratic method relies on him asking his listeners questions about common concepts, such as friendship, beauty, courage, temperance and piety, and then demonstrating through further questioning and reasoned argument that the answers he received were in some way inadequate or defective. It is a form of argument known as the *elenchus*, designed to identify and explore inconsistencies in beliefs.

An example makes the process clear. Plato tells us how Socrates once asked Laches, a celebrated Athenian general, what courage was. Confidently, Laches replied that it consisted of standing firm in battle. Socrates then pointed out that standing firm in battle is not necessarily courageous, as a foolish and reckless soldier might well stand firm, even though he could put others at risk by doing so. Therefore the definition was incorrect.

Condemned by the establishment

It was debates such as this that led the authorities in Athens to conclude that Socrates, although admired by the young aristocrats of the city, was fast becoming a dangerous and subversive influence. He was brought to trial, charged with impiety and corrupting Athenian youth. Socrates refused to bow to his judges, agree to stop philosophizing and retire into private life, which was probably all they wanted. He refused to recant or repent, was found guilty and ordered to put himself to death, which he did by drinking hemlock.

The authorities had their revenge, but Socrates's achievements survived him and them. His core beliefs – that no one who preserves their personal integrity can come to any long-term harm and that no one knowingly does wrong – stand as ethical beacons that have retained their importance right up to the present day, as has the Socratic method he devised.

ABOVE: **Socrates revolutionized Greek philosophy by trying to get at truth by persistent questioning, discussion and debate.**

23

Democritus

c.460 BC—c.370 BC

The last of the great pre-Socratic philosophers, Democritus originated the theory that the universe is made up of indivisible atoms that are constantly moving. He is often referred to as the 'laughing philosopher' because of the emphasis he placed on the value of cheerfulness.

Atoms

Only fragments of Democritus's writings survived beyond the Middle Ages, and much of what we know of his philosophy derives from the work of others, notably Aristotle and Diogenes Laertius. What makes him important in the development of Western thought is his assertion that countless indivisible atoms, which are constantly in motion and travelling in an infinite void, are the basic stuff of the universe. All that actually exists, he argued, are atoms and space. Equally, all material objects are simply temporary concentrations of atoms which are destroyed when the atoms disperse.

Pursuing knowledge

Democritus called the empty space he believed existed between the atoms the void. He argued that, despite what Parmenides and Zeno had previously postulated – that motion and hence the void cannot exist – movement must exist because it is an observable fact. Therefore there must be a void. This could not be thought of in the same way as material matter, rather it was merely the absence of matter. It was materially independent and had nothing to do with the existence of atoms.

Building on this, Democritus also held that there were two ways of knowing – one through the senses and the other through the power of the intellect. The former he classed as 'bastard' knowledge and the latter as 'legitimate'. For him, 'bastard' knowledge was knowledge obtained solely thought the five senses. Gaining 'legitimate' knowledge, on the other hand, relied on logical reasoning. He postulated that every event that occurs in the universe is casually determined by preceding events, asserting that he 'would rather discover one cause than gain the kingdom of Persia' – given that the Persian empire was unquestionably the richest and most powerful state at the time, this was an emphatic statement.

Teaching through maxims

As far as politics and ethics were concerned, Democritus relied heavily on maxims to make his point. 'Equality is always noble,' he stated – even though it seems he excluded women and slaves from the equation – while goodness, he believed, comes from practice and self-discipline rather than innate human nature. According to him, achieving inner contentment depends on living what he described as 'a measured life'. This, he wrote, was 'a state in which the soul lives peacefully and tranquilly, undisturbed by fear or superstition or any other feeling'.

❝ *Happiness resides not in possessions and not in gold, the feeling of happiness dwells in the soul.* ❞

Although at the time Democritus was something of a loner – he was largely ignored by his intellectual contemporaries in Athens with the exception of Plato, who so disliked his teachings that he called for his works to be burned – his theories had a major influence over subsequent generations of thinkers. Atomism, as Democritus's teachings came to be known, played a major part in shaping Epicurus's thought, so becoming one of the foundation stones of a whole philosophical system, which, together with Stoicism, was to come to dominate the culture of both the Hellenistic and Roman worlds.

Plato

c.427 BC−c.347 BC

The first Western thinker whose writings have survived intact, Plato, Socrates's favourite pupil, is generally regarded as one of the greatest philosophers of all time. No one has had a greater influence on the subsequent development of Western philosophical thought.

BIOGRAPHY

Name Aristocles, nicknamed Plato

Born c.427 BC

Place Athens

Nationality Greek

Key facts Plato's best-known doctrine is that, although the material world is defective and illusory, there exists another perfect one, populated by changeless entities called Forms. His writings blend ethics, political thought, moral psychology, metaphysics and epistemology into a systematic whole.

Died c.347 BC

KEY WORKS

• *The Republic*

• *Symposium*

• *Meno*

• *Theaetetus*

• *Parmenides*

The supreme philosopher

Plato travelled widely after Socrates's death, returning to Athens at the age of 40 to found his celebrated Academy in 385 BC. For many, he is the supreme philosopher. His influence on philosophical development is incalculable, in part perhaps down to his broad span of interests. Unlike the philosophers before him, he was not content to pursue knowledge only through discussion and debate. He was fascinated by the subject in its entirety.

The Theory of Forms

The doctrine for which Plato is probably best known is the so-called Theory of Forms. It is based on the notion that, in the material world, everything without exception is a copy of an ideal, unchanging Form, which has a permanent, indestructible existence outside the confines of time and space. In the everyday world, nothing lasts and nothing ever stays the same. By contrast, the world of the Forms is one in which there is permanence, order and ultimate reality.

Forms are blueprints. Plato argued, for instance, that, although there are countless cats, dogs and trees in the world, they are all made in the single universal Form of 'the cat', 'the dog', 'the tree'. Even men are made in the image of the universal Form of man. The key was the soul, which is immortal, existing even before birth. When the time comes to die, the soul is reincarnated into a new life form. As a result, so Plato postulates, all knowledge is recollected from a previous existence. He also believed that there were ideal Forms of universal, abstract concepts such as beauty, truth and justice, and of such mathematical concepts as number and class.

Rule by the few

Plato's theory coloured his entire view of human existence. In *The Republic*, probably his most celebrated work, what starts as an abstract thesis on the nature of justice soon becomes more politically and socially contentious. Plato sets out his vision of a Utopian society, ruled by an elite trained from birth for the sole task of ruling. The rest of society is divided into two lower orders – soldiers and the common people.

In Plato's Utopia there is no talk of personal freedom or individual rights. Everything is rigidly controlled by the guardians for the good of the state. As for the rest of the citizenry, their duty is simply to understand how best to put whatever talents they possess to work for the benefit of society as a whole and devote themselves solely to that task. Plato's state is certainly not a democratic one. Indeed, he openly condemned democracy as a source of bad government. This led later philosophers – notably Bertrand Russell – to accuse him of advocating totalitarianism. Counter-arguments have been made, but, whatever the truth, Plato's influence has been immeasurable.

ABOVE: **Plato founded his own Academy in Athens. His impact on Western philosophy is incalculable, particularly through the lasting influence he had on later Christian thought.**

Aristotle

384 BC−322 BC

Scientist, astronomer and political theorist as well as philosopher, Aristotle believed that everything is directed towards a final purpose. He is particularly renowned for inventing what is now called symbolic or formal logic and as the founding father of scientific method.

BIOGRAPHY

Name Aristotle

Born 384 BC

Place Stagira, Thrace

Nationality Greek

Key facts Aristotle made observation and the strict classification of data key elements of empirical science and is regarded as the founding father of true scientific method. He was the first of the great thinkers to study the nature of deduction and put its principles into use.

Died 322 BC

KEY WORKS

- *Physics*
- *Metaphysics*
- *Nicomachean Ethics*
- *Politics*
- *Poetics*
- *De Anima*

Advocate of empiricism

Aristotle is one of the most important figures in the early story of Western philosophy. His advocacy of empiricism as the only reliable philosophical method profoundly influenced medieval and later scholars.

Aristotle was sent to Athens at the age of 17 to enrol as a student at Plato's Academy. He remained there – first as a pupil and then as a teacher – for 20 years, until Plato's death, after which he left Athens and subsequently became the tutor to the young Alexander the Great. Returning to Athens some years later, he founded the Lyceum, his own philosophy school, where he taught until he was forced to flee following Alexander's death in 323 BC, dying in exile a year later.

He was the first great thinker to realize that, despite what Plato and the pre-Socratic philosophers had argued before him, it is impossible to devise a single, universal philosophical principle. Thus, he denied that there could be exact laws of nature, although he maintained that certain metaphysical categories – quantity, quality, substance and relation, for example – could be used in devising descriptions of all natural phenomena.

The Four Causes

To understand anything, Aristotle stated it was essential to analyse it empirically by asking four logical questions, termed the Four Causes: the Material Cause (what it is made of), the Formal Cause (what it is), the Efficient Cause (how it came to be) and the Final Cause (what it is for).

The Golden Mean

His aim was to develop a universal system of reasoning through which it would be possible to discover all that there is to be known about reality. Everything, he maintained, whether animate or inanimate, has a natural function, which it naturally strives to fulfil. This is its *telos* – its final purpose, or goal.

As far as humanity is concerned, its natural function is not simply to reason but to reason well. This is the key to the full development of human potential. According to Aristotle, tailoring human actions to accord with what reason dictates involves following what he famously termed the Golden Mean, the middle way between the two extremes of excess and insufficiency. Displaying true courage, for instance, means choosing the mean between foolhardiness and rashness on the one hand and cowardice on the other. Truthfulness consists of finding the mean between boasting and undue modesty. This applied as much to society as a whole as it did to individuals within it, and the primary function of the state was to make individual happiness possible.

Although knowledge of Aristotle's work died out in Europe during the Dark Ages, it was kept alive in the Muslim world and eventually made its way back in the late Middle Ages. There is no underestimating his significance, and his philosophy – notably his political, moral and aesthetic theories – has remained influential down to the present day.

❛ All human actions have one or more of these seven causes – chance, nature, compulsions, habit, reason, passion and desire. ❜

RIGHT: **Having studied under Plato for 20 years, Aristotle emerged as a great philosopher in his own right. Among his many other achievements, he was the inventor of symbolic logic.**

Epicurus

341 BC–270 BC

One of the most significant philosophers of his time, Epicurus argued that the gods have no influence on life, which should be devoted to the pursuit of happiness. His hedonism was widely denounced as flouting traditional morality.

BIOGRAPHY

Name Epicurus

Born 341 BC

Place Samos, Greece

Nationality Greek

Key facts Believed, with Democritus, that the basic constituents of the world are atoms and tried to explain all natural phenomena in atomic terms. He and his followers believed it was the duty of everyone to seek fulfilment by making the most of life.

Died 270 BC

KEY WORKS

• *Letter to Herodotus*

• *Letter to Pythocles*

• *Letter to Menoeceus*

Founder of Epicureanism

Although only three letters plus a list of maxims survive in a volume of Diogenes Laertius's *Lives of Eminent Philosophers*, they sum up his teachings well. Epicurus studied philosophy under followers of Democritus and Plato. In 306 BC, he arrived in Athens, where he founded the Garden, a combined school and philosophical community, whose members put his sociological and ethical teachings into practice. There are very few philosophical movements that owe their existence to a single thinker, but Epicureanism is an exception, as after Epicurus's death in 270 BC, Epicurean communities sprung up throughout the Hellenistic world. Together with Stoicism, it became the major philosophical influence of the day.

Pursuing pleasure

Although he followed Democritus, one of his teachers, in embracing atoms and atomism, his real interest lay in devising a practical philosophy of life. Happiness, he said, is the greatest good. It is only pleasure that is intrinsically valuable and only pain that is intrinsically bad.

According to Epicurus, there are two types of pleasure – 'moving' pleasures and 'static' pleasures. The first of these results from satisfying a desire – eating when hungry, for example. 'Static' pleasures occur when such a desire has been fulfilled. This type of pleasure, said Epicurus, is better than the first.

Defining desire

Just as there were two types of pleasure, Epicurus said there were various types of desire – natural and necessary desires, natural but unnecessary desires and what he labelled 'vain and empty' ones. Natural and necessary desires are the desire for food, shelter and the like. Vain and empty desires include those for riches, power and fame, which are practically impossible ever to satisfy because they have no natural limit. If a person is driven by the desire for wealth, it is probable that he or she will never be able to amass enough to satisfy it. Moreover, such desires are not natural ones. They are inculcated by society and by false notions of what we need.

Despite the later belief that he favoured hedonism, he advocated caution when dealing with natural but unnecessary desires. The wise, he said, strive to eliminate or avoid the pain and anxiety unfulfilled desires inevitably cause. Leading a peaceful, virtuous life is the key to achieving true *khara* (joy) as opposed to *hedone* (pleasure).

Under attack

Epicurus and his followers had to face substantial criticism. One reason for this was his rejection of the belief in an afterlife. He also disputed the notion that the gods actively concerned themselves with human affairs. If they were willing to prevent evil but were not able to do so, they could not be omnipotent; if they were able to do so but unwilling to do it, they must be malevolent. If they were both able *and* willing to do so, how could evil exist?

Early Christians attacked Epicureanism fervently, but later it revived, influencing the development of humanism and the beginnings of modern science.

BELOW: **Epicurus taught that men should devote themselves to the pursuit of happiness, which, he said, could be achieved by eliminating mental and physical pain.**

6 *Do not spoil what you have by desiring what you have not. Remember that what you have now was once among the things you hoped for.* 9

Marcus Aurelius

AD 121–180

Described by Edward Gibbon in The Decline and Fall of the Roman Empire *as 'the philosophic king', Marcus Aurelius was a noted Roman Stoic even before he became the ruler of Rome. He owes his reputation to his* Meditations, *a personal notebook containing advice on how best to live life the Stoic way.*

Heir to an empire

Marcus Aurelius's early education was overseen by the Emperor Hadrian; he was later adopted by the Emperor Antoninus Pius as his heir. He spent much of his reign fighting the barbarians, particularly in Central Europe, where he is thought to have written his *Meditations*. He was heir to an extremely influential tradition, which had been long established as a major philosophical force in republican and imperial Rome – Stoicism.

Cicero, Cato and Seneca were all Stoics, as was Epicetus, a former slave whose teachings greatly influenced the young Aurelius. Inner freedom was to be obtained only through submission to providence – the will of the gods – and cultivating detachment from anything outside one's personal control. Epicetus's twin maxims were to abstain and to endure. Marcus Aurelius shared these views. 'Does aught befall you? It is good,' he wrote. 'It is all part of the great web, which has been ordained for you since the beginning of time.'

Who were the Stoics?

Stoicism began in Athens around 300 BC and spread from Greece to Rome and then throughout the Roman world. The Stoics made bold claims. Everything, they argued, is governed by rational principles, so there are reasons for everything being the way it is. Things cannot be changed nor should anyone desire to change them. Anything that affects us is part of an unfolding divine purpose that it is impossible for us to influence or change. This is as it should be, for the plan is ultimately good.

Marcus Aurelius himself advised: 'Try living as a good man and see how you fare as one who is well pleased with what is allotted to him from the whole and finds his contentment in his own just conduct and kindly disposition.' In other words, virtuous people willingly accept their

lot, whatever it may be. Pleasure, pain, health, wealth, reputation, power and so on are all of no significance in themselves. They only become important when people judge them to be so and such judgements – if they run against reason – are invariably false. Marcus Aurelius warned: 'The happiness of your life depends on the quality of your thoughts. Therefore, guard accordingly and take care that you entertain no notions unsuitable to virtue and reasonable nature.'

Stoicism's influence

Marcus Aurelius was just one of the many rulers influenced by Stoicism and its principles, although he is particularly noteworthy. It is not surprising that the philosophy appealed to the governing classes, as the more people are willing to accept that things are as they should be, the less trouble they are likely to give.

   Stoic ethics also had an unmistakeable influence on early Christian ones, which were beginning to develop at the very time Marcus Aurelius was writing. Ironically, he backed the continuing persecution of the growing Christian population of the Roman empire, undoubtedly because the Christians posed a threat to the stability of the social order his philosophic principles told him he should protect.

ABOVE: **Ruler of the Roman empire from AD 161 to 180, Marcus Aurelius put his Stoic philosophical principles into action as he strove to govern imperial Rome at a time of growing political turbulence and military tension.**

Sextus Empiricus

AD 160–210

A shadowy figure about whom not much is known, Sextus Empiricus's reputation rests on the books he wrote outlining the nature of Pyrrhonic scepticism. When his work was rediscovered, hundreds of years after his death, it revolutionized the study of philosophy.

BIOGRAPHY

Name Sextus Empiricus

Born AD 160

Place Unknown

Nationality Greco-Roman

Key facts His reputation stems from *Outlines of Pyrrhonism*, an outline of the principles of a form of scepticism named after Pyrrho of Elis, and *Against the Dogmatists* and *Against the Professors*, sceptic criticisms of rival philosophies.

Died AD 210

KEY WORKS

• *Outlines of Pyrrhonism*

• *Against the Dogmatists*

• *Against the Professors*

Making a record

All we know of Sextus Empiricus's life is that he was probably Greek by origin – although some claim that he came from North Africa – that at some stage of his career he was a physician and that he was likely to have been a pupil of Herodotus of Tarsus, whom he succeeded as head of the sceptic school. He appears to have lived in Rome for some time and to have been acquainted with Athens and Alexandria.

What makes him an important figure in the story of philosophy is not so much his own thought – he was mainly a compiler rather than an original philosopher, drawing freely on the writings of his predecessors – but the authoritative record of the major school of philosophy he left behind him. Without this, we would know little or nothing about the sceptics and what they stood for and far less about many earlier Greek philosophers.

Sextus was a follower of Pyrrho, the founder of an extreme form of scepticism around the third century BC. Pyrrho and his disciples held that, in philosophy, there could be no such thing as certainty. Any philosophical argument or proof starts from a premise, which, by its very nature, is intrinsically not proveable. This led them to criticize other contemporary philosophical doctrines, notably those of the Stoics, Epicureans and the followers of Aristotle. Instead, they advocated suspending judgement. Such a suspension – *epoche* is the Greek term they used – leads to what they termed *ataraxia*, equanimity about what constitutes truth or falsehood.

Outlining Pyrrhonism

Sextus summed up the sceptic position in his *Outlines of Scepticism*. In it, he asserted that there was no means of proving anything one way or the other and how, by taking the sceptic route, it was possible to achieve peace of mind. By suspending judgement of what is right or wrong, true or false, good or bad, he argued, a true sceptic can become indifferent to the vicissitudes of life and so achieve inner tranquillity. 'By scepticism,' he wrote, 'we arrive first at suspension of judgement and second at freedom from disturbance.'

Sextus went on to discuss what he claimed was the folly of dogmatic and academic philosophical doctrine. Dogmatists, he said, assert truth is discoverable. Academics deny this. Sceptics avoid the extremes of both positions. In the six books that make up his *Against the Professors*, he criticized 'grammarians, rhetors, geometers, arithmeticians, astrologers and musicians' for making inherently false postulations and abstract suppositions.

ABOVE: **Empiricus argued that it was impossible to establish for certain whether or not anything was true.**

The sceptic legacy

Sextus was not without his critics. In the fourth century, St Gregory of Nazianzus denounced him together with Pyrrho for infecting people with a 'vile and malignant disease'. When, however, his work was rediscovered in the late 16th century it was to have a far-reaching impact on Western philosophical thought.

Tertullian

AD 160–220

A brilliant, sometimes controversial, thinker, Tertullian – Quintus Septimius Florens Tertullianus, to give him his full name – is known as the father of Latin Christianity for the innovations he introduced into its theology. He invented the term trinitas *(the Trinity) and is credited with helping to establish Latin as the vehicle for Christian thought.*

BIOGRAPHY

Name Tertullian

Born AD 160

Place Carthage

Nationality Roman

Key facts A brilliant, forthright Christian thinker, philosophically he was an extreme realist, having little time for the Greek philosophers who preceded him.

Died AD 220

KEY WORKS

- *Apologeticum*
- *De Praescriptione Haereticorum*
- *De Anima*

A Christian convert

What little we know of the details of Tertullian's life are that he was born in Carthage, the son of a Roman centurion, and was probably sent to Rome in his teens to train as a lawyer. After his return to his home city in around AD 197, he was converted to Christianity and emerged as a brilliant, sarcastic and sometimes aggressive writer, who soon carved out a name for himself as one of the leading Christian theologians of his day. According to contemporary accounts he was also a fine speechmaker. Of his many works, 31 survive, although some of these were corrupted in their copying or are not intact.

What makes Tertullian's philosophy interesting is his obsession with realism and his determination to avoid metaphysical speculation. He despised Plato, Aristotle and other Greek thinkers, scorning them for their inconsistencies. Even more importantly, rather than trying to reconcile their work with Christianity, he forthrightly condemned their teachings for inspiring heresy.

RIGHT: **Tertullian was a philosophical realist who despised metaphysics.**

Origen

AD 185–254

One of the most influential thinkers of the early church, Origen produced the first philosophical exposition of Christian doctrines and beliefs. Although he rigidly adhered to the teachings of the Bible in his philosophy, he was also influenced by Platonism. He argued that, as the Bible was inspired by God, its content was always right, even if it appeared to be in error.

Martyr philosopher

Origen lived during a turbulent period of Roman history, when barbarian incursions threatened the stability of the empire and Christians faced repeated persecutions under different emperors. Origen's own father, also a Christian, died a martyr's death, which goes a long way to explaining Origen's own fascination with martyrdom. He got his wish. He died after being tortured during a persecution.

Brought up in one of the principal intellectual centres of the ancient world, Origen was marked out from boyhood as one of the most promising members of Alexandria's intellectual elite. His father made sure that he was schooled in biblical studies and in Greek philosophy.

Philosophically, Origen's most important work is his treatise *Peri Archon*, which is generally regarded as the seminal exposition of what became known as Christian Neo-Platonism. Here, he set out his explanation of the nature of the Trinity and his view of human souls and the path that should be followed to ensure their redemption. Uniquely among his fellow Neo-Platonists he introduced history into his philosophy, while his insistence that all souls were absolutely free did much to counteract the fatalism that characterized the speculations of many of his contemporaries.

BIOGRAPHY

Name Origen

Born AD 165

Place Alexandria

Nationality Egyptian

Key facts A Neo-Platonic Christian thinker, Origen believed souls were free and not bound by the constrictions of fatalism.

Died AD 254

KEY WORKS

• *Peri Archon* (*On First Principles*)

LEFT: **A Christian who was martyred for his faith, Origen tried to reconcile the teachings of Plato with those of Christianity.**

Plotinus

AD 205–270

One of the most influential philosophers of ancient times after Plato and Aristotle, Plotinus is generally held to be the last great thinker of the Roman age. Developing Plato's mysticism, his achievement was to make Platonic philosophy central to Christianity's intellectual development.

A late developer

A pupil of Ammonius Saccas, an obscure philosopher in Alexandria, Plotinus did not begin studying philosophy until the relatively advanced age of 28. A decade or so later, he decided to study Persian and Indian thinking, but his plan to do so came to nothing when the Emperor Gordian III – to whose military expedition to Persia Plotinus had attached himself – was murdered by his own troops. The thwarted philosopher made his way to Rome instead, where he taught until shortly before his death.

Plotinus did not write much until relatively late in life, but when he did he more than made up for lost time. His many works were collected and edited by Porphyry, his favourite student, who gave the collection the title *Enneads*, from the Greek word for nine, thus reflecting the fact that there are nine treatises in each of the six books in the collection.

The three levels

Building on Plato's belief that ultimate reality consisted of Ideal Forms, Plotinus developed the premise that everything that exists is fundamentally mental. He went on to argue that there were three levels of reality: in ascending order, the Soul, the Intellect and, finally, the One. The human task, he held, was, through contemplation, to progress logically from one level to another and achieve union with the One.

Again taking his lead from Plato, Plotinus sometimes refers to the One as 'the Good', the mystical source of all reality, which can be only grasped indirectly by deducing what it is not rather than what it is. Below it comes the Intellect, which corresponds to infinite knowledge, the purpose of which is twofold. Firstly, it contemplates the *dunamus* (power) of the One, which it recognizes as its source, and, secondly, it meditates on its own thoughts, which Plotinus identifies with Plato's

Forms. Just like sunlight, he says, it illuminates the One. It is also the means by which the One contemplates itself.

The third and lowest level of reality is the Soul, which Plotinus subdivides into higher and lower divisions. According to him, the higher part is unchangeable and divine, while the lower part is the seat of the personality and hence of passions and vices. All human beings can choose to focus on the lower level and the material world, or they can look inwards and contemplate the higher realities of the Intellect.

Plotinus was in no doubt about which of the alternatives to choose. As reported by Porphyry, his last words as he lay dying were: 'Strive to bring back the God in you to the God in the All.' Christian thinkers later translated this and Plotinus's other dictates to suit their own thinking. The universe, they postulated, was created in the mind of God. Human beings naturally aspire to oneness with God, who, by definition, is the epitome of the good.

ABOVE: **Plotinus believed there were three divinities – the Soul, the Intellect and the One. It was the One, he postulated, that was the source of all reality.**

St Augustine

AD 354–430

Arguably the greatest philosopher of the period between Aristotle and St Thomas Aquinas, Augustine successfully fused Christian belief with the Platonic philosophical tradition. He held that, philosophically, it was possible to attain true wisdom only through God and religious faith.

Discovering Neo-Platonism

BELOW: **A cynic who became a devoted Christian, St Augustine believed it was only possible to attain wisdom through faith.**

As a young man, Augustine studied in Rome, Carthage and Milan. Having been reconverted to Christianity at the age of 28, he later returned to North Africa to found a monastery, becoming Bishop of Hippo in AD 395. One of the most powerful personalities in the entire history of philosophy, Augustine's central tenet was that rational thought had to be the servant of faith.

He quoted the prophet Isaiah – 'Unless thou believe, thou shalt not understand' – in support of this. The single most important moment in his philosophical development was when he first discovered the writings of the Neo-Platonists after becoming the Municipal Professor of Rhetoric in Milan when he was in his early thirties. Exactly which books these were is uncertain, but there is no underestimating the extent of their influence on Augustine's thinking. They provided him with the vital metaphysical framework on which he could build his own thought.

The written legacy

Augustine was a prolific writer, but his two greatest works were unquestionably his semi-autobiographical *Confessions*, written in around AD 400, and *The City of God*, which he began writing about AD 413 and finished in AD 426. Much of the former is an account of his somewhat chequered career before his reconversion to Christianity. The last three chapters are devoted to an explanation of the first book of Genesis and a philosophical analysis of the nature of time. For God, Augustine says, nothing is future or past. He does not exist within and is not bound by time; he is everlasting, eternal and beyond temporal constraint.

The City of God is universally regarded as Augustine's greatest work, written after Rome had been sacked by the Visigoths in 410. He originally intended it to be a rebuttal of those who then 'began to blaspheme against the true God more ferociously and bitterly than before', but his purpose soon became broader. What the book ended up as was, in part, a cogent argument against believing in any religion or philosophy other than Christianity and a cogent retelling of the biblical version of human history. Augustine saw this in terms of a constant conflict between what he refers to as the City of God (those preselected by God for salvation and who live their lives according to Christian values) and the City of Man (those who have strayed from the true path). Along the way, he tackles such knotty issues as original sin, free will and predestination.

Augustine's influence on the development of human thought was lasting and profound. In medieval times, Boethius, John Duns Scotus, Anselm of Canterbury and St Thomas Aquinas were all deeply influenced by what he had written. So, too, were other thinkers, such as René Descartes, Nicolas Malebranche and, more recently, Ludwig Wittgenstein – although Wittgenstein was concerned more with how Augustine described the learning of language than his purely philosophical speculations, such as how it was only through reasoning that faith's tenets could be proved and that rational thought was the servant of faith not its master.

BIOGRAPHY

Name St Augustine

Born AD 354

Place Thagaste, North Africa

Nationality Roman

Key facts His most important philosophical achievement was to marry Christian beliefs with the teachings of Plato and Plotinus, making the latter an integral part of Christian thinking.

Died AD 430

KEY WORKS

• *Confessions*
• *The City of God*

The Middle Ages

AD 500–1400 The fall of the Roman empire in the West
led to the Dark Ages and a consequent decline in European learning,
reflecting the troubled and barbaric nature of the times. Many of the
writings of the ancient thinkers were lost in the consequent turmoil
– for example, the only works of Aristotle to survive in Europe were his
thoughts on logic.

By contrast, the Muslim world preserved the learning Europe had lost.
Eventually, however, philosophy revived in the West, thanks largely to
the emergence of such thinkers as Duns Scotus, Anselm of Canterbury,
Peter Abelard and, above all, St Thomas Aquinas.

For Aquinas, theology was a science. Carefully applied reason,
he believed, could yield the demonstrable certainty of theoretical
knowledge. Like his fellow philosophers, he dedicated himself to an
overriding purpose: to reconcile philosophical speculation with the
tenets of the Christian religion and, through reasoning, prove the
existence of God.

Avicenna (Ibn Sina)

AD 980–1037

Nicknamed by his contemporaries al-Sheik al-Rais (Leader Among the Wise Men), *Avicenna was one of the foremost thinkers of the golden age of Muslim philosophy. He held that everything owed its existence to a First Cause and that the all-powerful creator had to be God.*

BIOGRAPHY

Name Avicenna (Ibn Sina)

Born AD 980

Place Afshana, near Bukhara, modern Uzbekistan

Nationality Persian

Key facts Philosophically, he attempted to combine Islamic theology and elements from Neo-Platonism with the teachings of Aristotle to produce a comprehensive theory about the nature of reality.

Died 1037

KEY WORKS

• *The Book of Healing*

The sole creator

Avicenna was a polymath. By the age of ten he had memorized the entire Koran, and by the time he was 21 he was an expert in all fields of learning, including mathematics, astronomy, logic, music and medicine. According to his autobiography, Avicenna based much of his philosophy on a mixture of what he learned through study and what he postulated through personal intuition. As a Muslim, he attempted to link the elements he drew from the teachings of Aristotle and Plato and reconcile them with the Muslim belief that God was the sole creator, the originator of everything that has existed, exists or will exist.

Avicenna's main contributions to philosophy were his *Philosophy for the Prosodist*, his first survey of metaphysics, and four massive encyclopaedic treatises: *The Book of Healing*, *The Book of Knowledge*, *Pointers and Reminders* and *The Judgement*, the last of which has been lost.

Of these, *The Book of Healing* was the most immediately influential. In it, Avicenna produced extensive surveys of logic, mathematics, the natural sciences, music and metaphysics, drawing on what he had found in Aristotle and the other Greek thinkers he had studied to develop his argument that God was the source of all things, the First Cause from which everything sprang. God, he reasoned, is the Necessary Existence.

> ❛ *The knowledge of anything, since all things have causes, is not acquired or complete unless it is known by its causes.* ❜

Knowledge, reason and logic

There was, said Avicenna, only one way that human beings could acquire knowledge and so come to a closer understanding of the nature of their creator. This was through the use of reason, the application of the five senses and the use of logic.

Of these, logic was the key to gaining true knowledge and developing understanding – as it was essential in knowing how to verify whether a proposition was true or not – and he explained how best this could be achieved through the use of formal and, more importantly, syllogistic inference.

Syllogisms

A syllogism contains two premises and a conclusion. A typical example runs as follows: all mortal things die; all men are mortal things; all men die. The secret, said Avicenna, is to identify the so-called middle term, the term that both premises have in common. In this case, it is 'mortal things'. Avicenna held that, by developing an understanding of such matters, human beings – or, at least, some of them – could eventually get in touch with the pure intellect that is God.

Avicenna's influence was immense. In the Islamic world, his work had an immediate impact, and in medieval Europe, too, knowledge of his works spread – largely through the translations of his writings into Latin that first appeared in Spain – informing the teachings of such influential Christian figures as St Thomas Aquinas.

ABOVE: **Avicenna came to the conclusion that the originator of existence could only be God. He argued that God was the First Cause, from which everything else sprang.**

45

St Anselm of Canterbury

1033–1109

Archbishop of Canterbury for 16 turbulent years and the outstanding Christian philosopher and theologian of his day, St Anselm is best known for the ingenious ontological argument he put forward to prove that God must exist, developed solely through the use of reason.

BIOGRAPHY

Name St Anselm of Canterbury

Born 1033

Place Aosta

Nationality Burgundian

Key facts His basic tenet was that, because the concept of God exists, it is self-evident that God exists as well.

Died 1109

KEY WORKS

• *Monologion*

• *Proslogion*

Fides quarens intellectum

Little is known of Anselm's early life before he entered the school attached to the great Benedictine abbey at Bec in Normandy in 1060. Within three years, he became the abbey's prior and, in 1078, its abbot. By this time he had written his *Monologion* and *Proslogion*, the two treatises for which he is best remembered and in which he attempted to prove the existence of God. Anselm became Archbishop of Canterbury in 1093.

Anselm's philosophical motto was *fides quarens intellectum*, or 'faith seeking for understanding'. It was this that inspired and drove his quest to prove conclusively that belief in the existence of God did not depend simply on the acceptance of scriptural teachings or doctrinal precepts but could be deduced through the power of reason. Eadmer, the scholar who later wrote Anselm's biography, put it neatly: 'Being continually given up to God and spiritual exercises, he [Anselm] attained such a height of divine speculation that he was able by God's help to see into and unravel many most obscure and previously insoluble questions.'

Anselm's aim was clear. He wrote in his prelude to the *Proslogion* – the word roughly translates as 'discourse' – that his plan was to show 'that God truly is, and that he is the supreme good'. The result was his development of what later became known as the 'ontological argument' for God's existence. It was to become one of the most hotly debated arguments in the history of philosophy.

Proving God exists

In his first attempt at devising a means to prove the existence of God, Anselm put forward several hypotheses. By the time he came to write the *Proslogion*, however, he had refined his views. He now held that God exists simply because the concept of God exists. Suppose, he argued, that the term 'God' is synonymous with a single supreme being. He is a being, Anselm postulated, of which nothing greater can be conceived.

Anselm constructed the rest of his argument as follows. He, he said, could conceive of such a being. It is also greater to exist in reality than simply in the imagination. Therefore, the being of which he conceived must exist in reality. The argument is ingenious, simple and cogent.

Attackers and defenders

Even in his own day, Anselm had his critics. Chief among them was Gaunilo of Marmoutiers, a Benedictine monk, who was deeply critical of Anselm's reasoning. Gaunilo claimed that it allowed for the existence of a host of supposedly perfect things that reason dictated simply could not exist. Anselm's reply was that it was a mistake to apply his reasoning to argue for the existence of anything other than God.

In the 18th century, Immanuel Kant, who coined the term 'ontological argument', was equally critical. He stated that Anselm's assertion was fatally flawed because existence could not be claimed to be perfection. Nevertheless, other philosophers – notably St Thomas Aquinas, René Descartes and, in modern times, the American philosopher Norman Malcolm – devised their own versions of Anselm's original argument.

BELOW: **St Anselm, (third from left) devised the ontological argument to prove the existence of God. He postulated that God must exist, as the concept of God exists.**

Peter Abelard

1079–1142

Famous as a poet, composer and the lover of the scholar and abbess Héloïse as well as a philosopher, Abelard was brilliant, innovative and controversial. He is best known for his contributions to metaphysics, language and logic, in particular for his advocacy of what came to be known as nominalism.

BIOGRAPHY

Name Peter Abelard

Born 1079

Place Le Pallet, near Nantes

Nationality French

Key facts A nominalist philosopher whose beliefs brought him into conflict with the church, Abelard was considered by many to be the greatest logician of his age.

Died 1142

KEY WORKS

- *Dialectica*
- *Theologia*
- *Ethica*
- *Sic et Non*

Debater and disputer

The son of a knight, Abelard chose not to follow in his father's footsteps, deciding instead to devote himself to a life of scholarship. Abelard's initial fame as a philosopher stemmed from the series of public disputations he entered into with his teacher, the realist William of Champeaux, in which he put himself forward as the champion of nominalism. This in itself was a controversial step to take, since it set him firmly on a collision course with many older, more traditional thinkers of the day, and his subsequent career was stormy. Although his forthright views won him a fanatical following, his teachings were twice condemned as being heretical.

Nominalism versus realism

The issue that divided the nominalists and the traditionalists – the realists as they became known – revolved around the problem of what, in philosophy, are termed 'universals'. These are words like 'red' or 'tree' that can be applied in exactly the same way to an infinitely large number of different objects. The question both groups tried to answer was whether or not such terms could also describe something with an independent existence of its own.

Realists were followers of Plato. Like him, they asserted that there were Ideal Forms – in the case of 'red', for instance, there was an Ideal Form of redness and the particular redness of each red object is a copy or reflection of it. The nominalists held the contrary view. Like Aristotle, while admitting that red objects obviously exist they denied that redness could exist independently as the realists claimed. Abelard stated the case succinctly. In his view, universals were simply *nomina* (words); the realist postulation was irrational and incoherent. Universality, he concluded, was simply a semantic feature of language and nothing more.

Condemned by the church

Abelard was the master of every kind of dialectical argument. The same applied when it came to logic – indeed, many hold him to have been the greatest logician of his time. However, when he attempted to employ logic and dialectic as tools to help him to develop his theological arguments, he ran into trouble with the church. Eventually, he was hauled before two church councils, one at Soissons and the other at Sens. The first ordered Abelard to ceremonially burn his *Theologia Summi Boni* in public. The same thing happened at the second, although this time it was a revised version of the *Theologia* that had to be destroyed. More seriously, however, Abelard was excommunicated.

He announced his intention of appealing directly to the pope, but before he could set out for Rome, Pope Innocent II lifted the excommunication. However, the sentence he substituted was equally harsh: Abelard was ordered to keep silent for the rest of his life. He died soon afterwards, but his work survived to influence the thinking of later generations of Western philosophers.

Averroes (Ibn Rushd)

1126–1198

The last and most influential of the great Muslim philosophers, Averroes fused Greek ideas, notably those of Aristotle, with Islamic thinking. He aimed to prove that philosophy and religion are not opposed, arguing that if two truths cannot contradict one another, there could be no conflict between the truths revealed by philosophy and those of religion.

Rediscovering Aristotle

Having followed family tradition by studying law, Averroes then took up medicine and philosophy, eventually becoming court physician to Abu Yaqub Yusuf, Caliph of Cordoba. Broadly speaking, Averroes made three important contributions to philosophy. His authoritative commentaries on Aristotle contributed greatly to the rediscovery of the great Greek thinker's works in the West, following centuries of near oblivion. In *The Incoherence of the Incoherence*, a counterblast to *The Incoherence of Philosophers* by the 11th-century theologian al-Ghazali, he successfully defended philosophy against attack. He condemned those who, like al-Ghazali, believed that philosophy should not concern itself with religious matters, all the ancient Greek thinkers should be ignored as they were pagans and, in any event, that it was impossible to employ philosophy to demonstrate key metaphysical truths.

Finally, Averroes constructed his own version of Aristotelianism, cleansing it, as far as possible, from any Neo-Platonist influences he saw as potentially corrupting. However, his enthusiasm for the work of ancient, non-Muslim thinkers made him many enemies among the more conservative and orthodox, and he was found guilty, on a trumped-up charge, of heresy and banished from the court and his writings ordered to be burned. Although he was pardoned, he died in exile shortly afterwards.

Learning from the past

Averroes's starting point was simple. The Koran, he said, actually advocated the study of philosophy. He cited verses such as 'Reflect if you have a vision' and 'They give thought to the creation of Heaven and Earth' in support. He went on to argue that, in order to discover the truth – philosophical and theological – it was essential to consult the works of the ancient philosophers such as Aristotle. 'All that is wanted in an inquiry into philosophical reasoning,' he wrote, 'has already been perfectly examined by the ancients. All that is required of us is that we should go back to their books and see what they have said in this connection. If all that they say be true, we should accept it and, if there be something wrong, we should be warned by it.'

Averroes built on what he had learned from Aristotle and others with what he found in the Koran to formulate his own view of the universe. There were two reasons, he postulated, why God must exist. Everything in the universe served the human purpose. For this to be so there had to be a creator, and this had to be God. Similarly, everything in the world was designed, which implied the existence of a designer. This, too, had to be God, who, said Averroes, is the eternal prime mover, around whom everything else revolves.

Averroes's influence on philosophy was profound. Paradoxically, though, he lived at a time when interest in philosophy was waning in the Muslim world just as it was reviving in Christendom, thus explaining why his speculations had more influence on Christian and Jewish thinkers than on his co-religionists.

RIGHT: **Averroes** believed that there was only one truth and that, rather than being in conflict, theology and philosophy were both converging on it.

Moses Maimonides

1135–1204

Medieval Judaism's foremost intellectual, Maimonides was a skilled physician – he was court doctor to the great Saladin – and a brilliant theologian. In his philosophy, his aim was to reconcile any contradictions between philosophical tenets and those of the Bible.

BIOGRAPHY

Name Moses Maimonides

Born 1135

Place Cordoba

Nationality Jewish

Key facts Scholar and physician as well as great thinker, Maimonides suggested that while not everything in the Bible should be taken literally, human reasoning could not contradict the truth as revealed by God.

Died 1204

KEY WORKS

• Guide for the Perplexed

Fleeing from persecution

Maimonides had a turbulent upbringing. His family was forced to flee from Spain to escape religious persecution – first to Morocco and then to Cairo, where he settled for the rest of his life. By the time he arrived, he had already begun work on his massive 14-volume commentary on the Torah, which, when it was published, immediately established him as one of the great Jewish thinkers of the day. In it, he attempted to demonstrate that every part of Jewish law served a rational purpose, a brilliant analysis that delved right to the heart of Jewish religious belief.

Reconciling teachings

From theology, Maimonides turned to philosophy, although, in his mind, the two subjects were inextricably linked. In 1190 he completed the *Guide for the Perplexed* (*Moreh HaNevuchinin*), his most important philosophical work. It took the form of a letter of advice written to one of his students who was unable to decide whether to follow the precepts of Greek philosophy or to abide strictly by the teachings of the Jewish religion. In it, he asserted that, despite the teachings of Aristotle, whom he deeply admired, there were fundamental limits to the extent of human knowledge. It was impossible for any truths arrived at through human reasoning to contradict those revealed by God.

Deeply influenced by his own study of Aristotle, although he rejected some of his teachings, Maimonides himself believed that there were few, if any, major contradictions between the two points of view. He pointed out, for instance, that *ma'aseh bereishit* (the account of the beginning) in Jewish tradition paralleled what the ancient Greek thinkers taught about physics. Similarly, what Jewish tradition taught as *ma'aseh merkavah* (the account of Ezekiel's chariot) was similar to what the Greeks taught as metaphysics. Knowledge was the key to finding true wisdom and fulfilling the biblical commandment to love God. He also argued that

the biggest obstacle to achieving this goal was to fall into the trap of interpreting everything in the Bible literally. This, he warned, opened the door to idolatry.

However, when it came to trying to describe God, Maimonides was an advocate of what was termed the *Via Negativa*, or negative theology, which suggested that the only way God could possibly be described was through negative attributes. It would be incorrect, for instance, to say that He exists; all that can be safely said is that He is not non-existent. Maimonides concluded that what he termed God's 'essence' was indefinable and unknowable.

These and some of Maimonides's other contentions aroused substantial opposition among his more conservative Jewish contemporaries, who particularly criticized him for the way in which he rejected literal interpretation of the Bible. For this reason, his writings were banned in some orthodox circles. Nevertheless, his work proved to be remarkably influential on later thinkers, including St Thomas Aquinas, Baruch Spinoza, Gottfried Leibniz and Sir Isaac Newton.

ABOVE: **The pre-eminent intellectual figure of medieval Judaism, Maimonides was instrumental in reintroducing Aristotle's ideas back into Western philosophy. Later, Spinoza was indebted to Maimonides as the source of some of his notions.**

St Thomas Aquinas

1225–1274

Unquestionably one of the greatest of all medieval thinkers, St Thomas Aquinas was noted both as a philosopher and a theologian. At the heart of his thought lay his personal belief that Christian teaching could be reconciled successfully with the dictates of science and philosophy.

BIOGRAPHY

Name St Thomas Aquinas

Born 1225

Place Roccaseca

Nationality Italian

Key facts In his teachings, which later became embodied in a philosophy called Thomism, St Thomas Aquinas attempted to reconcile Aristotelian and Christian thinking while maintaining the distinction between faith and reason.

Died 1274

KEY WORKS

- *Summa Contra Gentiles*
- *Summa Theologica*

Defining 'natural law'

Born into the aristocracy, St Thomas Aquinas was educated by the Benedictines before moving on to attend universities in Naples and Cologne and to teach theology in Paris. Against the wishes of his family, he finally became a Dominican friar. His output was vast – he produced more than eight million words during his lifetime – and all of it is important. Like Aristotle before him, he believed that everything had a purpose. What he added to this was that this purpose – of everything animate or inanimate – was given to it by God. The universe and everything in it was imbued with divine purpose. It followed from this that, by studying the world carefully, looking into the essential nature of things and the laws that governed what each was for, it was perfectly possible to determine what God's plan and intentions were for his creation.

This applied as much to human beings as it did to everything else. Aquinas theorized that humanity was created by God for a purpose. By probing into our essential natures and so discovering this purpose, we can establish what God intends us to be. By becoming aware of what is in keeping with God's intentions and what runs counter to them, it becomes clear what is morally good and bad. Philosophers call this theory 'natural law.'

The 'Five Ways'

The belief that everything had a purpose was by no means the only idea Aquinas adopted from Aristotle. He also held the view that all rational knowledge was acquired through sensory experience on which the mind could then reflect. For this reason, much of Aquinas's thinking was profoundly empirical, although he was careful to set limits on what empiricism could achieve as opposed to the insights that resulted from divine revelation. In the first part of his *Summa Theologica* (*Summary of*

Theology), perhaps his most influential work, he employed deductions based on pure reason to produce five different, albeit interrelated, proofs to demonstrate the existence of God. His conclusion was that God was unquestionably the Prime Mover, the universal First Cause without whom nothing could exist.

After offering his proofs of God's existence and discussing his various attributes, Aquinas set out his views on ethics. The human task was clear. It was to strive towards what he defined as the highest ends. He devoted the final part to an examination of Christ, and he explains that Christ is not only the source of human salvation but represents and protects humanity both in Heaven and on earth.

Aquinas never finished *Summa Theologica*, however. Why he suddenly stopped writing it is unclear. According to his own account, some four months before his death he experienced some form of cathartic religious experience during mass: 'All that I have written seems to me like straw, compared to what has now been revealed to me.' He never picked up a pen again.

BELOW: **St Aquinas held that everything had a God-given purpose and that rational knowledge could be acquired only through sensory experience.**

John Duns Scotus

1266–1308

Nicknamed 'the subtle doctor' by his contemporaries, the Scottish Franciscan friar Duns Scotus – or John Dun the Scot, as he is more properly known – is thought by some to be one of the greatest metaphysicians that ever lived. In part, his philosophy was a reaction against the teachings of St Thomas Aquinas and Aristotle.

BIOGRAPHY

Name John Duns Scotus

Born 1266

Place Duns

Nationality Scottish

Key facts Scotus's argument for the existence of God is considered an outstanding contribution to philosophical theology. He is also noted for his explanation of universals and his belief in free will.

Died 1308

KEY WORKS

• *Ordinatio*

A wandering philosopher

Little is known about the details of Scotus's life. He was born in 1266 in a village just a few miles from the Scottish–English border and taught at Oxford before moving to Paris and then to Cologne, where he died suddenly and prematurely in December 1308. What is clear is that his meticulous, closely reasoned and often extremely complex philosophical thought won him a considerable reputation among his contemporaries. Understanding his work today is hard, since most of what survives of his writings exists only in the form of the notes he made for his many lectures, and *Ordinatio*, which is generally regarded as his most significant contribution to the subject, is basically a revised version of notes he made for lectures he delivered at Oxford University. He began it soon after leaving Oxford in 1302 and continued to work on it intermittently until his death.

Does God exist?

Scotus's crowning achievement was to devise an extremely complex metaphysical argument to demonstrate that God *must* exist. He argued that the existence of God could be proven only by arguing more or less backwards from its effects, so that it can only be inferred rather than positively postulated.

He also speculated about natural law, which, for him, in its broadest sense, is simply the expression of God's will. God wills certain propositions to be; thus they are law. Because God can do anything that is not logically impossible, whatever He wills is, by definition, right.

Unlike St Thomas Aquinas – some of whose teachings he and his followers criticized – Scotus was not a fully fledged Aristotelian, although some of his thinking was nevertheless influenced by his work. In particular, Scotus insisted that nothing could be known without the

> *The will of God is illuminated by the divine intellect and the primacy of the will of God does not negate the natural order which is valid also in God.*

ABOVE: **John Duns Scotus reacted against the ideas of St Thomas Aquinas and Aristotle, arguing that nothing can be known without the assistance of divine revelation.**

benefit of what he termed 'divine illumination'. Even with its aid, however, there were only three modes of knowing that did not require further proof: principles that could be established by *a priori* reasoning; things that become known through experience; and, finally, the knowledge people gain by their own actions.

Individuation

Scotus was also concerned with the principle of individuation. This has several meanings, but, in philosophy, it is generally held to describe the development of the individual from the general or universal and the distinction or determination of the individual within the general and universal.

According to Scotus, what individuates one thing from another must depend on form rather than matter. It was impossible to individuate two things by claiming that they were different substances or in different places; it was possible to do so only by taking account of their attributes or qualities and how these were combined. Nor can any two objects ever possess the same combination of attributes. To defend himself against the criticism that this was demonstrably incorrect, Scotus qualified his argument by saying that it was only in form and not in substance that things can be told apart – thinking that later influenced the work of Gottfried Leibniz and other eminent philosophers.

William of Ockham
c.1288–c.1348

Best known for devising the famous principle known as 'Ockham's razor', which states that, in cases where there is a choice between two theories, the simpler of the two is more likely to be correct, William of Ockham was a radical who pioneered a new, empirical philosophical approach.

BIOGRAPHY

Name William of Ockham

Born c.1288

Place Ockham

Nationality English

Key facts William of Ockham argued for cutting out complexity in favour of simplicity. 'It is vain,' he was reported as saying, 'to do with more what can be done with fewer.'

Died c.1348

KEY WORKS

• *The Sum of Logic*

Dogged by controversy

Very little is known about William's early life – there is even some dispute as to whether he was born in Ockham in Surrey or the village of the same name in Yorkshire. At some stage, he was ordained as a Franciscan friar and studied and taught at Oxford, although he never took a degree.

His life was controversial, not so much on account of his sometimes radical philosophy – although his forthright views attracted considerable criticism – but because of his embroilment in a quarrel within the Catholic church. It started in 1327, when William was ordered to leave Oxford and journey to the court of Pope John XXII in Avignon to investigate the charge of heresy that had been laid against Michael of Cesena, the head of the Franciscan Order to which William belonged. He found for his master against the pope, and papal retaliation was swift. William was excommunicated in 1328 after he fled Avignon without permission. He finally found sanctuary at the court of Ludwig of Bavaria, where he remained until his death, probably a victim of the Black Death.

William and the church were never reconciled before he died. He had not helped his case by attacking St Thomas Aquinas with a destructive criticism of the synthesis between faith and reason that Aquinas had striven hard to create. William maintained that belief in God had to be a matter of faith not of knowledge. Consequently, he rejected all the attempts that previous philosophers had made to use reason to prove God's existence.

Ockham's razor

William produced other radical arguments that ran counter to contemporary trends in medieval philosophical thinking. He asserted, for instance, that there were no such things as universals. Reality is composed ultimately of simple singulars, created by God, and which survive independently. In other words, no single thing depends on anything else

for existence. Change was simply the reordering and rearranging of these singulars. As for such supposed universals as 'redness', 'species' and even 'humanity', these were purely human inventions.

In some ways, William's vision of reality anticipated the logical atomism of Bertrand Russell and the early thought of Ludwig Wittgenstein many centuries later. However, what he is best remembered for is the invention of the methodological principle now universally referred to as 'Ockham's razor', which posits that, if there are two possible explanations that are equally effective in explaining the same data, the more complicated one is likely to be wrong and the simpler one correct. 'Entities', he warned, 'should not be posited unnecessarily.' In other words, assuming that all other things are equal, why postulate more than one thing when one will do?

ABOVE: **William of Ockham postulated that it was only by observation and through experience that we can gain real knowledge of the natural.**

The Early Modern Era

1400–1800 With the coming of the Renaissance, philosophy changed dramatically. Previously, the great thinkers had tested their speculations and postulations chiefly through discussion and argument. Now, hand-in-hand with the birth of modern science, philosophy became more scientific as new savants started to test their theories scientifically.

Many philosophers came to the belief that the key to gaining knowledge of the world was through reason, and they came to be known as rationalists. The French philosopher René Descartes was foremost among them, followed by the Dutchman Baruch Spinoza and the German Gottfried Leibniz. All three used mathematical principles to devise new ways of understanding the world.

The empiricists – the likes of John Locke, George Berkeley and David Hume – disputed the rationalist dogma. They held that all knowledge was derived from the sensory experience, and this principle has influenced most philosophical thinking in the English-speaking world ever since.

Niccolò Machiavelli
1469–1527

Although he published just a single significant treatise – Il Principe (The Prince) – Machiavelli is arguably the world's best-known political theorist. Because of the methods he advised his ideal ruler to employ, his name has become a byword for political chicanery and skulduggery.

Diplomat turned thinker

The son of a Florentine lawyer, details of Machiavelli's early life are sketchy until 1498, when, after the overthrow of Florence's ruling regime, he emerged as a leading administrator in the new Florentine republic, which he served mainly as a diplomat for 14 years. During this time he amassed the knowledge that he was to embody later in his political thinking. Machiavelli fell out with the republic, however, and although he dedicated *The Prince*, his manual of statecraft, to Lorenzo de Medici, the head of the family that now ruled the city, he was never to regain any political power.

The Prince

Machiavelli's lasting legacy stems from his authorship of *The Prince*, in which he defines his ideal ruler and details what such a ruler must do to secure and hold on to power. The unscrupulous methods Machiavelli suggested his prince was perfectly justified in employing have made his name synonymous with nefarious political machination, giving rise to the term 'Machiavellian'. Such a ruler's first duty, Machiavelli argued, was to do anything it took to secure and maintain power, even if that meant overriding customary moral convention. 'A man who wishes to make a vocation of being good at all times will come to ruin among so many that are not good,' he warned. 'Hence it is necessary for a prince who wishes to maintain his position to learn how not to be good and to use this knowledge or not to use it according to necessity.'

Ruling through fear

In advocating such an approach, Machiavelli ran counter to the accepted philosophical thinking of his times, which held that rulers should strive to be morally and ethically virtuous. He held that it was better to be feared and respected rather than loved by one's subjects, just as violence and deception were superior to legality when it came to controlling them effectively. 'Men', he wrote, 'are less hesitant about harming someone who makes himself loved than one who makes himself feared ... Love is a bond of obligation that these miserable creatures break whenever it suits them to do so. But fear holds them fast by a dread of punishment that never ceases.'

Appearing virtuous

However, Machiavelli also believed that it would be counterproductive to indulge in cruelty for its own sake. On the contrary, even though his ideal ruler had to be ready to cheat, torture and murder if the situation demanded it, such a ruler, he said, should always appear to be a paragon of virtue. 'A prince', he wrote, 'ought to take care that he appears to him who sees and hears him as altogether merciful, faithful, humane, upright and religious.'

Anything, it seemed, could be justified in the pursuit of what Machiavelli classed as the three primary political goals: strong government, security and national independence. His precepts have never dated and are as relevant today as they were in Renaissance Italy.

❝ One can say this in general of men: they are ungrateful, disloyal, insincere and deceitful, timid of danger and avid of profit. ❞

Michel de Montaigne

1533–1592

In his time, de Montaigne was admired more as a polished writer than as a deep thinker. Nevertheless, the reflections in his Essais *proved to be of major importance, influencing other philosophers, including René Descartes, Jean-Jacques Rousseau and Ralph Waldo Emerson.*

BIOGRAPHY

Name Michel de Montaigne

Born 1533

Place Saint-Michel-de-Montaigne

Nationality French

Key facts A humanist and a sceptic, Montaigne relied on his own judgements. The only sure way of gaining knowledge, he argued, was through experience and the ability to reflect on one's own thoughts and actions.

Died 1592

KEY WORKS

• *Essais*

Humanist and sceptic

Montaigne's wealthy father masterminded his son's education, making sure that he grew up not only reading but speaking Latin fluently. Although Montaigne eventually became Mayor of Bordeaux, his chief occupation from the age of 37 onwards was his writing. In all, he compiled three volumes of essays in which he applied his governing philosophical principles to a huge variety of topics.

Unlike the majority of his contemporaries, Montaigne was more interested in speculating on how he and other humans related to one another and the world around them than trying to explain man's relationship with God. He started from the precept that it was impossible to be certain about anything, while too much knowledge could prove to be a burden. He and his fellow thinkers must exercise 'free judgement' and avoid accepting any belief uncritically.

Free judgement

Lamenting that 'even with people of understanding, philosophy should be an empty and fantastic name, a thing of no use and no value', Montaigne rejected speculative philosophy as practised by many of his contemporaries as unsound. He argued instead for the development of a whole new approach in which scepticism had a vital part to play. Believing that knowledge was just as likely to stifle understanding as to promote it, his aim was to liberate thought from the straightjacket of false certainty. A thinker's task was to balance continually one opinion against another, using one's own judgement to test them for veracity. For him, philosophy could never be a science; it was simply a way of life.

This scepticism had profound implications. He argued, for instance, that there were no good reasons for saying that human beings were better than other species, since there were no universal standards to enable a valid judgement to be made as to which was superior. Indeed, he postulated such standards were completely unnecessary, although he conceded that the idea of them – notions such as 'reason' and 'nature' – could help people to exercise their judgement better.

The same argument applied to cultures. In his essay 'On Cannibals', Montaigne contended that there was no reason to suppose that Western culture was closer to God, goodness and truth than other, supposedly less advanced cultures. Individuals, he said, should think about and then evaluate the customs they lived by, and then, if necessary, challenge them.

Montaigne's thinking, especially his scepticism, inspired many later thinkers, notably Blaise Pascal and René Descartes. The latter, in particular, was impressed by Montaigne's belief in the importance of self-education. Like Montaigne, Descartes taught himself more or less from scratch, following his predecessor's advice on how to achieve independence and firmness of judgement. Much more recently, Claude Lévi-Strauss hailed him as the father of cultural relativism, while his approach to philosophy inspired such influential modern sages as Richard Rorty to look for new ways of seeking out knowledge and truth.

BELOW:
Montaigne was a key Renaissance philosopher noted for coining the motto 'what do I know?' Certainty, he said, was impossible to establish.

Sir Francis Bacon

1561–1626

In the period between the Renaissance and the early modern era, Francis Bacon was a key figure in the development of true scientific method. His chief contribution was to father a new empirical form of inductive reasoning, based solely on observation and experiment.

BIOGRAPHY

Name Sir Francis Bacon

Born 1561

Place London

Nationality English

Key facts Bacon, the father of modern scientific methodology, attacked the belief that scientific truth could be established through argument; only the new approach he advocated could advance knowledge and establish scientific truth.

Died 1626

KEY WORKS

• *Novum Organum*

• *On the Dignity and Advancement of Learning*

• *The New Atlantis*

Inventing scientific method

The youngest son of Sir Nicholas Bacon, Lord Keeper of the Great Seal for Elizabeth I, Bacon became an important political figure while still finding the time for philosophical speculation. He rose to prominence under James I, eventually becoming Lord Chancellor, but, soon after his appointment, he was accused of taking bribes, fined, imprisoned and banished from the royal court. Although James later pardoned him, it was the end of his political career.

More importantly today, he was the pioneer of modern scientific method. Claiming that 'knowledge is power', he dedicated himself to the wholesale reform of the traditional methods of scientific investigation, proposing the establishment of an entirely new system, which, he claimed, would open the way to discovering real knowledge 'for the use and benefit of men'.

Bacon started by tearing to pieces the efforts of the two schools of thought that hitherto had dominated philosophical and scientific inquiry. The rationalists, who believed that knowledge could be acquired by close examination of the content and meaning of words, were dismissed out of hand. They resembled, he said, 'spiders, which make cobwebs out of their own substance'. The Aristotelians, in his view, were no better. All they did, he contemptuously commented, was run around like ants to amass raw data, which they had no idea how to interpret meaningfully.

Instead, Bacon advocated a novel, even revolutionary, way of thinking. 'The greatest change I would introduce,' he wrote, 'is in the form of induction, which shall analyse experience and take it to pieces, and, by a due process of exclusion and rejection, lead to an inevitable conclusion.' He believed that science, if properly understood, offered humanity its best possibility of understanding the natural world and, by so doing, becoming master of it.

Experiment and hypothesis

There was an intriguing twist in Bacon's reasoning. What he advised investigators to do was to strive not only to prove their hypotheses by means of experiment but also not to be afraid of disproving them. Even negative results, Bacon advised, could be valuable. If a hypothesis is correct, by definition it cannot contain any negative instances. Therefore, a negative result is the only way of knowing for certain that an assumption is false. He also counselled investigators to avoid the 'idols' he warned were otherwise likely to distort their thinking. These can best be described as tendencies or defects of the mind that can combine to stop the development of total understanding.

There can be no questioning Bacon's importance. No less a luminary than Karl Popper, one of the key philosophers of the 20th century, readily admitted his debt to Bacon and his work. Without him and the methods he pioneered, it is unlikely that science as we understand it would even exist.

ABOVE: **Bacon, a true Renaissance figure, championed the use of inductive reasoning as the only way to establish knowledge and truth.**

Thomas Hobbes

1588–1679

One of the most influential political philosophers of all time, Hobbes was, by nature, something of a pessimist. He believed that without the imposition of a binding social covenant between man and an omnipotent state, human life would be 'solitary, poor, nasty, brutish and short'.

The universe as a machine

Hobbes studied at Oxford before becoming tutor to William Cavendish, scion of the wealthy and well-connected Cavendish family. His post gave him the opportunity to travel around Europe, where he met some of the greatest philosophers of the day. A Royalist supporter, he went into exile during the English Civil War, returning home in 1651, having reconciled himself to Oliver Cromwell's rule.

As a political thinker, Hobbes was a materialist. 'The universe, that is the whole mass of things that are,' he said, 'is corporal, that is to say body, and hath the dimensions of magnitude, namely length, breadth and depth … every part of the universe is body and that which is no body is no part of the universe. And, because the universe is all, that which is no part of it is nothing and consequently nowhere.' Only matter existed. Like other 17th-century thinkers, he subscribed to the 'corpuscular theory', which holds that the material world is made up of tiny, invisible corpuscles. It is their texture and movement that explains the behaviour of the objects they make up. Building on these beliefs, Hobbes concluded that the universe was a vast machine, and everything in it, including man, was an integral part of the machinery.

Covenant and contract

Hobbes was a negativist. Perhaps his thought was coloured by what was going on in the world around him: in England, Charles I was at war with Parliament, while on the Continent, the Thirty Years War was raging.

What Hobbes believed was that, in what he termed the 'state of nature', people were driven by the need to satisfy their natural desires, whatever the cost. Everyone would 'do what he would to possess, use and enjoy all that he would, or could, get'. The inevitable result was conflict and war. In the 'state of nature', Hobbes warned, there was 'no society; and, which is worst of all, continual fear and danger of violent death'.

man and state. For this to work, the state would have to be absolute. Once it had been entered into, the covenant, naturally, would need to be enforceable, by the sword if necessary; covenants 'without the sword are but words'. There was no alternative to complete submission to 'that great Leviathan, or, rather, to speak more reverently, that mortal God, to which we owe under that immortal God our peace and defence'.

These views were radical. They were also unpopular. Nevertheless, the notion of a social contract has had many defenders, although most hold it to be implicit rather than explicit. Few, however, have followed Hobbes in going to such extremes.

argued that only an absolute government could ensure the preservation of order in society.

René Descartes

1596–1650

Often referred to as the father of modern philosophy, Descartes set the speculative agenda for thinkers for at least three centuries. He started from the premise that the only certainty is one's own existence, a belief that led him to coin the maxim cogito ergo sum: *I think therefore I am.*

In search of certainty

Descartes was educated by the Jesuits and at the University of Poitiers before fighting in the armies of Maurice of Nassau in the Netherlands and Maximilian of Bavaria. On retiring from soldiering, he started on a new career as a thinker, although he first won fame as a mathematician – he invented analytic geometry – and a natural scientist before emerging as the most important philosopher of his day.

As a philosopher, Descartes was influenced substantially by the certainty he found in mathematics. This, he reasoned, was because of the deductive methods mathematicians used to reach their conclusions, and he wondered whether it might be possible to apply the same logical method to other disciplines. Although he was not a sceptic as such, he employed scepticism freely as a vehicle to motivate his questioning of each and every one of his beliefs. His aim was to find which, if any, of them was infallible. If one was not, he could be certain that it and any other belief derived from it would be unreliable and had therefore to be excluded.

Cartesian deduction

Descartes's first step was to question the value of direct, immediate observation. He concluded that it was worthless and so rejected any information obtained through the senses as uncertain and fallible. A wise thinker, he said, never trusts that which once deceived him. He went on from this to hypothesize that it is possible, on occasion, to be dreaming what we see. Dreams, said Descartes, can seem just like waking life, at least at the moment of their dreaming. As there are no criteria to help us distinguish being awake from being asleep, how can we be certain that we might not have dreamed the truth of any belief we hold to be true? It is another logical reason for doubting any beliefs based on the evidence of the senses. There might even be a malicious demon at work, putting all sorts of ideas and experiences into our heads with the deliberate intention of deceiving us.

His conclusion was that practically all his beliefs were open to doubt. There was one, however, about which he felt secure. When he was thinking, it must be the case that he exists, for he must exist in order to be able to think. This postulation provided him with the one indubitable truth he sought. Based on it, he started to construct a whole new belief system in such a way that doubt could not creep back into it through the back door.

Whether Descartes succeeded in this ambition is open to question. Undoubtedly, his work gave birth to a new school of philosophy known as rationalism, which is based on the postulation that knowledge of the world can be acquired only through the use of reason. Many modern philosophers, however, argue that the problems Descartes posited remain unresolved. It is easier, they say, to destroy belief than to restore or resurrect it.

❛ Except our own thoughts, there is nothing absolutely in our power. ❜

LEFT: **Descartes believed that all knowledge had to be deduced through the use of reason. The only thing that is certain, he said, is personal existence.**

Blaise Pascal

1623–1662

An infant prodigy who, in his short life, made significant contributions to philosophy, mathematics, physics and theology, Pascal is best known for the famous wager he devised concerning the existence of God.

BELOW: **Pascal believed that scientific knowledge grew from generation to generation, but believing in the existence of God, though rational, would always remain a matter of faith.**

Scientist and philosopher

Pascal was a gifted mathematician and scientist, who devised his first mathematical proof at the age of only 11. He turned to philosophy after becoming involved with the religious movement known as Jansenism.

In 1647, after four years of research, Pascal published his *Experiments on a Vacuum*, in which he demolished the prevalent Aristotelian view that 'nature abhors a vacuum'. He went on to outline the principles of a new scientific methodology. Science, he said, should be a progressive enterprise with succeeding generations of scientists building on the

knowledge passed on to them by their predecessors. 'It is in this manner that we may at the present day adopt different sentiments and new opinions ... without despising the ancients and without ingratitude, since the first knowledge which they have given us has served as a stepping stone to our own.'

Pascal's wager

When it came to religion, however, a different set of rules came into play. After his dramatic conversion to Christianity and his continued involvement with Jansenism, Pascal became committed to the Christian cause. He fully accepted the Augustinian belief that the expulsion of Adam and Eve from the Garden of Eden marked the fall of man, leaving humanity spiritually corrupt to the core. Ultimate salvation could come about only through the will of God.

Nevertheless, traces of the old rationalism can still be found in his religious thinking, notably his celebrated wager, which he included in his *Pensées*, the apologia for Christianity he left unfinished on his death. Since, he argued, the question of whether or not God existed could not be settled definitely one way or the other, the best that could be done was to wager as to which view was correct. If God does exist, the reward for the believer is eternal bliss. If He does not, there is little really lost. For the unbeliever, if God exists, the reward is eternal damnation, while, if He does not, there is little really gained. Pascal argued that belief was by far the more sensible wager: 'I should be much more afraid of being mistaken and then finding out that Christianity is true,' he wrote, 'than of being mistaken in believing it not to be true.'

Decision theory

The wager is not is an argument for the existence of God, rather it is an argument for the rationality of belief. It has had its critics. Some say, for instance, that we cannot choose what we believe, while others claim that it is based on several dubious assumptions, that the arguments for and against God's existence are evenly balanced, for example. Additionally, some would suggest that Pascal was wrong to assume all believers will be rewarded with eternal bliss, while, conversely, all unbelievers will face eternal damnation. Would God not see through someone who believed in him purely for convenience's sake on the basis of a self-interested calculation? Or, if God is all forgiving, how can Pascal be so sure that all unbelievers inevitably face damnation?

Despite such criticisms, Pascal's wager is still seen by many as an influential philosophical argument. It is one of the earliest examples of what is termed 'decision theory'.

BIOGRAPHY

Name Blaise Pascal

Born 1623

Place Clermont, now Clermont-Ferrand

Nationality French

Key facts Influenced by the scepticism of Michel de Montaigne, Pascal argued that realism could only work from first principles, but it could not establish whether such principles were true.

Died 1662

KEY WORKS

• *Summa Logica*

Baruch Spinoza

1632–1677

One of the three most significant rationalist philosophers – the others being René Descartes and Gottfried Leibniz – Spinoza formulated an entirely novel theory concerning the nature of reality.

BIOGRAPHY

Name Baruch Spinoza

Born 1632

Place Amsterdam

Nationality Dutch

Key facts Spinoza was a pantheist, and the central tenet of his philosophy is that the universe and everything in it is one substance, which can be conceived of as either Nature or God.

Died 1677

KEY WORKS

- *Tractatus Theologica-Politicus*
- *Ethics*

Denounced by the church

The son of Jewish parents who fled to the Netherlands from Portugal to escape the Inquisition, Spinoza was himself excommunicated from the Jewish faith for 'abominable heresies' and 'monstrous deeds'. Later, he was to be denounced by Christians, too, as an atheist and his books burned in public. Perhaps part of the problem was, although he believed God was literally everywhere, he failed to stick to religious orthodoxy.

Spinoza is generally thought of as being one of the most compelling of all the rationalist philosophers. In his thinking he took rationalism to its logical extremes, dismissing the notion of sense perception as a valid means of acquiring knowledge and substituting for it a purely intellectual form of cognition. In moral philosophy, the naturalistic view he took of God, the world and his fellow human beings provided a firm foundation for his belief that controlling passions was the key to finding the way to virtue and happiness.

In life, Spinoza was something of a loner. He turned down the offer of a professorship at the University of Heidelberg in order to preserve his independence. Instead, he combined philosophy with making a living grinding lenses for spectacles, telescopes and microscopes. The daily inhalation of powdered glass over the years may well have contributed to the development of the lung disease that caused his relatively early death.

> ❝ *I have made a ceaseless effort, not to bewail, not to scorn human actions, but to understand them.* ❞

Ethics

Spinoza produced only one book under his name – the rest of his writings appeared anonymously. *Ethics*, his undoubted masterpiece, was published posthumously. It is a complex work. First, it is not just about ethics; it sets out Spinoza's entire theory of the nature of reality. Second, it is a difficult read. This, in part, is because of the way Spinoza deliberately structured it to resemble a geometrical proof.

Rejecting Descartes's view that mind and matter were separate substances, each capable of existing independently, Spinoza believed that everything was made up of a single unitary substance that possessed an infinite number of attributes. Human beings, he said, can only be aware of two of these: physical extension and thought. These do not possess a separate reality; they are simply aspects of the One, which can be conceived of either as Nature or as God. God, said Spinoza, is infinite and all encompassing. Everything is a part of Him, and everything that happens is a necessary expression of the divine nature.

Unorthodox views

Such views were decidedly unorthodox. So, too, was Spinoza's explanation of evil, which he said did not exist, at least in the accepted religious sense. Things that seem to be evil appear so only because of a lack of understanding of the chain of causes that makes all events a necessary part of the divine reality. Nor do human beings possess souls. These and similar propositions ran directly counter to the central tenets of the Christian faith, which is why Spinoza decided to postpone the publication of *Ethics* once he had completed the great work.

His philosophical reputation today is mixed. Although his thoughts on metaphysics have been largely discounted, modern philosophers still consider his ethical ideas relevant.

BELOW: **Spinoza was a philosophical loner who turned down a professorship to preserve his independence.**

John Locke

1632–1704

Regarded by many as the founding father of empiricism, Locke was one of the most important thinkers of his time. He advocated the notion of a social contract between citizens and the state, arguing that the former had the right to rebel against a government ruling without its consent.

BIOGRAPHY

Name John Locke

Born 1632

Place Wrington

Nationality English

Key facts Locke denounced authoritarianism and the divine right of kings, arguing that a ruler could rule only with the consent of the governed. Philosophically, he held that all knowledge is derived ultimately from experience.

Died 1704

KEY WORKS

• *Two Treatises of Government*

• *An Essay Concerning Human Understanding*

The first empiricist

Locke lived through turbulent times. His father, a Puritan, fought for Parliament in the English Civil War, and Locke himself, after completing his studies at Oxford, became personal physician to the Earl of Shaftesbury, one of the leaders of the parliamentary opposition to the Stuart monarchy. Eventually, Locke fled to Holland to avoid arrest, returning a decade later after James II's overthrow in 1688.

He was undoubtedly a thinker of the first rank, distinguishing himself both as a political theorist and as a pure philosopher seeking to define the limits of human understanding. His claim to philosophical fame rests on his *An Essay Concerning Human Understanding*, published in 1690. It was the culmination of 20 years of reflection on the origins of human knowledge.

Locke's aim was ambitious. It was, he wrote, 'to examine our own abilities and see what objects our understandings were, or were not, fitted to deal with'. Other outstanding figures in philosophy later followed him along the same lines of inquiry: David Hume, Immanuel Kant, Arthur Schopenhauer, Bertrand Russell, Ludwig Wittgenstein and Karl Popper rank among their number.

His conclusions were remarkable. There were no such things as innate ideas. At birth, the human mind is a *tabula rasa*, a blank slate. All that we learn subsequently we discover through external perception, utilizing the five senses. It follows logically from this that all knowledge is derived ultimately from experience, either coming directly from the senses or constructed out of elements that are derived from them. 'No man's knowledge here,' Locke concluded, 'can go beyond his experience.'

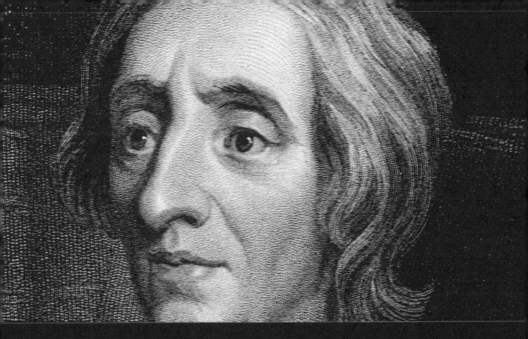

Revolutionary implications

The implications of this were revolutionary. If, as Locke argued, everyone started life with a clean slate mentally, no one person could be born superior to another. Everything depended on how the individual was educated. This led many, especially in France, to the conclusion that, through education, the mass of the people could be liberated from social subjugation. Such reasoning would have come as no surprise to Locke, since he was just as interested in political theory as he was in pure philosophy.

At the same time as he was working on his essay, he was also setting out his political thinking in his *Two Treatises of Government*. Here, Locke agreed with Thomas Hobbes that humanity begins in a state of nature; it is in what happens afterwards that the two thinkers differ. Although both men advocated the conclusion of a freely agreed social contract and the consequent setting up of a government, Locke, unlike Hobbes, said that the governed still retained their individual rights even after government had been established. For Locke, sovereignty rested ultimately with the people. If their rights were to be attacked or not defended effectively, they had the moral right to rise in rebellion, overthrow their government and replace it with a new one. Locke's argument still has potent political force.

ABOVE: **Locke argued that all knowledge must be derived ultimately from experience and the evidence provided by the senses of sight, hearing, smell, taste and touch.**

Gottfried Leibniz

1646–1716

Leibniz was a master of metaphysics and a pioneer of mathematical logic. He is noted for devising the principle of sufficient reason, which holds that nothing happens without a reason, and formulating Leibniz's law, which states that identical things must share the same properties.

The eternal optimist

Leibniz was the son of a professor of moral philosophy at the University of Leipzig. As a philosopher, he was an optimist, and at the heart of his thinking lay the belief that, because it was created by God, this world must be the best of all possible worlds.

Reality, he argued, consisted of an infinite number of unities, which he christened 'monads'. They are, he wrote, 'the real atoms of nature and, in a word, the elements of things'. This view helped to make Leibniz's philosophical reputation, even though *Monadology*, the book containing it, was not published until after his death. His principle of sufficient reason became equally celebrated. Put at its simplest, it postulates that, for everything that is the case, there must be a reason why it is the case.

Leibniz's law is just as famous. Essentially, it states that, if two objects are identical, they will be indiscernible; that is, they will not differ in their properties. It is a law that has retained its importance in philosophy right up to the present.

ABOVE: **In addition to philosophy, Liebniz made major contributions to technology, medicine and politics.**

George Berkeley
1685–1753

An Irish scholar who formulated his most important thinking as a young man before becoming an Anglican cleric and ultimately a bishop, Berkeley won renown as the father of so-called 'philosophical idealism'. He held that only minds and spirits, and not matter, exist.

A young idealist

Berkley did practically all his significant philosophical thinking before the age of 30 while a fellow of Trinity College, Dublin. He went on to become Dean of Londonderry, visited America, where he hoped to set up a seminary in Bermuda, and, finally, after his return, was appointed Bishop of Cloyne.

Berkeley's major philosophical concerns were twofold: he wanted to find a way of dealing with the sceptics and their view of the material world; and he was also determined to counter what he saw as a growing philosophical tendency to put God at the periphery when speculating about the nature of the world. As a devout Anglican, Berkeley believed it was his duty to bring God back to centre stage.

Philosophically, Berkeley was an idealist. Everything that exists, he held, is either a mind or depends on a mind for its existence. Even common physical objects, he argued, are composed solely of ideas, which are inherently mental. His ideas were certainly thought provoking. They were also unorthodox, running counter to the philosophical trends of his times.

BIOGRAPHY

Name George Berkeley

Born 1685

Place Kilkenny

Nationality Irish

Key facts Berkeley argued that there was no such thing as matter, and his most celebrated dictum was *esse est percipi*; to be is to be perceived.

Died 1753

KEY WORKS

- *Treatise Concerning the Principles of Human Knowledge*

- *Three Dialogues Between Hylas and Philonous*

LEFT: **Berkeley attacked materialist mathematicians like Newton who expected 'an undue deference to their decisions where they have no right to decide'.**

79

Voltaire

1694–1778

Francois-Marie d'Arouet – Voltaire as he is universally known – was one of the giants of the 18th-century Enlightenment. Deeply influenced by the philosophy of John Locke and Sir Isaac Newton, he championed reason over ignorance, intolerance, bigotry and religious superstition.

Rejecting the establishment

Voltaire was born into a well-to-do aristocratic family. Educated by the Jesuits – he later claimed to have learned nothing from them but 'Latin and the Stupidities' – his first ambition was to succeed as a playwright, to the dismay of his father, who was a prominent official at the court of Louis XIV. Eventually, he established himself as a man of letters, turning to philosophy while in voluntary exile in England. On his return to his homeland, he took the side of Newton against Descartes in the great debates that, for many years, split French philosophical thinking. He also fiercely attacked Gottfried Leibniz for what he saw as his fatuous philosophical optimism.

Perhaps the most explosive and potentially revolutionary philosophical notion that Voltaire propounded was Locke's belief that, rather than being innate, knowledge comes solely from experience. Through his determined advocacy of this principle, Voltaire did more to initiate what became known as 'the age of reason' than any other thinker. Alongside his championship of empiricism, he called for an end to the abuse of power by the social elite and for the right of everyone to freedom of expression.

Attacked and persecuted

Given his fiery pen and the fervency with which he articulated his beliefs, it is scarcely surprising that at times throughout his long life Voltaire had to face fierce persecution by the establishment. The church found him particularly vexatious. Although at heart he was a deist, believing in a creator God, Voltaire came to be regarded by almost everyone as the champion of revolutionary freethinking. He believed, he wrote, that 'religion does not consist either in the opinions of an unintelligible metaphysic, or in vain display, but in worship and justice'. It was a distinctly unpopular view.

Voltaire's liberal politics were treated with equal suspicion by the Bourbon government. Even though for a time Frederick the Great of Prussia was one of his patrons, his denunciations of authoritarianism and his calls for reform made him many powerful enemies. As he said: 'One questions every day whether a republican government is preferable to a king's government.'

Philosophical principles

Philosophically, Voltaire's thinking revolved around a single master theme, the right of everyone to enjoy personal liberty. This was one of the reasons he was such a champion of empiricism and such a determined opponent of dogmatism and the pernicious authority he felt that it engendered.

It was important, too, for a philosopher to be sceptical. Voltaire denounced what he contemptuously termed 'philosophical romances', in other words, philosophical explanations that, although supposedly systematic, ultimately overcame doubt only by appealing to the human imagination. This was why, in his satirical novel *Candide*, he was so critical of Gottfried Leibniz and his doctrine that this world, created by a rational God, is the best of all possible worlds. Rather than advocate what he derisively described as 'mataphysico-theologo-cosmolonigolgy', a philosopher, Voltaire stated, needed to recognize that often the most philosophical explanation is to offer no explanation at all.

David Hume

1711–1776

The last of the great British empiricists, Hume, whose work is still highly influential, began his philosophical career early but won recognition only after his death. He was one of the most important exponents of philosophical naturalism and a precursor of modern cognitive thinking.

BIOGRAPHY

Name David Hume

Born 1711

Place Edinburgh

Nationality Scottish

Key facts Better known as an economist and historian than a philosopher during his lifetime, his *Dialogues Concerning Natural Religion* created a sensation when it appeared posthumously.

Died 1776

KEY WORKS

- *A Treatise of Human Nature*
- *Enquiry Concerning Human Understanding*
- *Enquiry Concerning the Principles of Morals*
- *Dialogues Concerning Natural Religion*

The ultimate empiricist

Although Hume's greatness as an original thinker is now undisputed, during his lifetime his philosophy won very few adherents. This may have been because many of his contemporaries simply failed to understand it. Arguably only two of them, Immanuel Kant (who said it was Hume's philosophy that woke him from his 'dogmatic slumbers') and Thomas Reid, came anywhere near grasping its conclusions.

Hume was a child prodigy who entered university when aged only 11. After graduating, he moved to France, where for three years he worked on *A Treatise of Human Nature*, which he published at the age of 28. 'It fell dead-born from the press,' he lamented, 'without reaching such distinction as to even to excite a murmur among the zealots.'

Hume was the ultimate empiricist. Following the teachings of John Locke, he argued that any knowledge not based on experience was, by definition, false and had to be ruthlessly discarded. His conclusion was that, apart from mathematics, it was impossible to know anything for certain unless it first could be proved empirically.

Cause and effect

To be justified in claiming that anything exists, Hume said, we have to be able to provide evidence for its existence through observational experience. If there is none – as Hume famously argued when debating the existence of God – then the thing cannot exist. He used the same argument when dealing with the problem of causality – that is, the relationship between cause and effect. Hume pointed out that causal connection cannot be observed and so must be considered inherently unreliable.

What most people believe is causation – one thing happens as the result of another – is simply a form of what philosophers term 'inductive reasoning'. It is making an assumption based on observing a number of similar instances. So if, for example, a person observed many white swans but no black ones, they might conclude that all swans are white. In fact, according to Hume, generalizations like this cannot be justified. Logically, no matter how many times something is observed, there is always the possibility that next time something different will occur.

Living by assumption

Given that we cannot be sure of anything, Hume argued for the adoption of what he referred to as 'mitigated scepticism'. He postulated that the best we can do is to assume that, in fact, there are connections between things, although it was impossible to prove their existence. He called on people to 'reject every system, however subtle or ingenious, which is not founded on fact and observation' and to 'hearken to no argument but those which are derived from experience'. The 'airy sciences' of the metaphysicians, he argued, should be abandoned in favour of a more pragmatic, utilitarian approach.

Hume's speculations deeply influenced philosophers through the 19th century and continue to be debated right up to the present day. Some modern philosophers believe that some of the basic concerns he raised – notably the whole issue of inductive reasoning – are as yet unresolved.

BELOW: **Hume was an extreme empiricist, arguing that all knowledge had to be gained from the senses.**

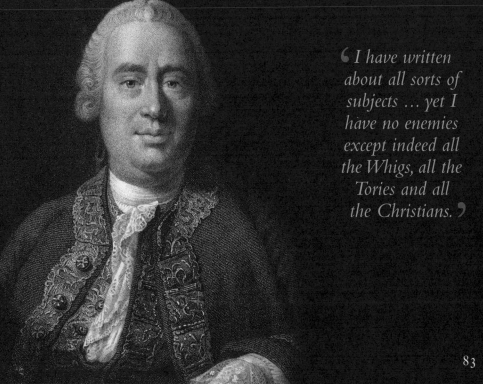

❛ I have written about all sorts of subjects … yet I have no enemies except indeed all the Whigs, all the Tories and all the Christians. ❜

Jean-Jacques Rousseau

1712–1778

The son of a watchmaker, Rousseau rose from his relatively humble beginnings to become one of the most important figures in the history of political philosophy. In his greatest work The Social Contract, *he argued for the establishment of an ideal society in which man would finally be freed from his chains.*

Distrusting civilization

BELOW: **Rousseau distrusted what civilization had done to man, arguing that people could be free only in a natural uncivilized state.**

In his mid teens Rousseau left Geneva for France, becoming the protégé of Madame de Warens, an influential baroness, who paid for him to finish his education. His first major philosophical work, *A Discourse on the Sciences and Arts*, won him the prestigious essay prize of the Dijon Academy, after which he swiftly emerged as a leading figure in French intellectual circles.

Rousseau profoundly disliked and distrusted the way a supposedly civilized society had evolved and condemned what he felt man had become as a result. 'Man was born free,' he wrote, 'and everywhere he is in chains.' Civilization was not a force for good, as practically all his contemporaries believed; it was positively harmful. He considered that man, in a state of nature, was a 'noble savage'. Men in such a state 'do not know good or evil, but only their independence. The peacefulness of their passions and their ignorance of vice prevents them from doing ill.' He recognized it was impossible to turn the clock back – things had gone too far for that – but what, he wondered, could be done to free humanity from the psychological shackles of a corrupting civilization?

The social contract

Rousseau believed the answer was obvious: it was 'to find a form of association which will defend and protect with the whole common force the persons and goods of each associate, and which each, while uniting himself with all, may still obey himself alone and remain as free as before.'

What Rousseau was advocating was a new social contract, which he believed would serve as the blueprint for the ideal society. A root-and-branch reformation would transform the civilization he distrusted so much into an entirely new form of state, one in which liberty went hand-in-hand with law, freedom and justice.

Such a state would be ruled by what he called an 'elective aristocracy', a picked cadre of leaders periodically elected by the citizenry as a whole. Citizens would be raised and educated so that they identified themselves with the interests of the state, willing to vote for what Rousseau defined as the common good rather than being tempted to promote their own self-interests. For the same reason, such a state would not tolerate the existence of inequalities in social class and material wealth. The watchwords would be 'liberty, equality, fraternity'.

Legacy

Rousseau's ideas have had a lasting impact, being championed by the leaders of the French Revolution and influencing Immanuel Kant and Karl Marx. Some philosophers, however, have pointed out that there is a major flaw with what Rousseau advocated so passionately. In his ideal state, no individual has any right to deviate from the general will. If anyone does, 'he will be forced to be free' – in other words, to comply. Some have taken this to mean that Rousseau was advocating a form of totalitarianism where individual rights are sidelined when they conflict with the views of the majority.

Adam Smith

1723–1790

Often identified as the father of modern capitalism – he called it 'commercial society' – Adam Smith is famous for his advocacy of the free-market economy and his belief that 'unintended consequents of intended actions' will be of benefit to society as a whole.

BIOGRAPHY

Name Adam Smith

Born 1723

Place Kirkcaldy

Nationality Scottish

Key facts Smith's theories in *The Wealth of Nations* laid the philosophical foundations for 19th-century Britain's economic and industrial expansion and once again came to the fore in the political shake-ups of the 1980s.

Died 1790

KEY WORKS

- *The Theory of Moral Sentiments*
- *The Wealth of Nations*

Winning fame in his lifetime

Like his friend David Hume, Adam Smith was a leading member of the so-called *literati*, the group of thinkers who did much to create what became known as the Scottish Enlightenment. Unlike Hume, however, Smith won fame in his lifetime. *The Theory of Moral Sentiments*, his first major work, was a bestseller; *The Wealth of Nations*, which advocated the merits of free trade, choice and competition, provided the philosophical foundations for Britain's extraordinary economic and industrial expansion during the 19th century.

Smith was Professor of Moral Philosophy at the University of Glasgow when he wrote *The Theory of Moral Sentiments*. In it, he outlined the natural principles he believed governed human morality and the ways in which we come to know them. People, he suggested, are born with an innate moral sense, just as they are born with inherent notions of beauty or harmony. 'However selfish man may be supposed,' he wrote, 'there are evidently some principles in his nature, which interest him in the fortunes of others, and render their happiness necessary to him, though they derive nothing from it except the pleasure of seeing it.' We all possess an innate conscience, which is bolstered by natural fellow feeling – which he called 'sympathy'.

> ❛ *No society can surely be flourishing and happy of which the far greater part of the members are poor and miserable.* ❜

86

The Wealth of Nations

It was *The Wealth of Nations*, however, that proved to be Smith's masterpiece, winning him undying philosophical renown. Although frequently thought of as a study of economics, it is far more than that. It is a heady mixture of philosophy, economics, political science, history, sociology and even anthropology. Smith himself saw his book as a 'very violent attack upon the whole commercial system of Great Britain', by which he meant the mercantilism – the theory that a nation's wealth is rated by the amount of goods and money within its borders at any given time – and protectionism that dominated the economic thinking of the day. His contention was that it was labour that created wealth. Labour, he averred, was 'the only universal as well as the only accurate measure of value, or the only standard by which we can compare the values of different commodities at all times.'

Free trade and a free market

Smith argued that free trade was essential for the wealth created by labour to be increased. 'The more trade a country engages in, the wider the market becomes and the more potential there is for the creation of additional wealth.' The market, however, must operate freely without check or interference. Smith called this 'natural liberty'.

What Smith wanted to see created was 'universal opulence which extends itself to the lowest ranks of the people.' Nevertheless, his views have come in for substantial criticism. Despite the obvious value of some of his propositions – he argued in favour of better education for all, for instance – many believe that unchecked capitalism is exploitative and creates far more problems than it solves.

ABOVE:
A philosopher who speculated about economics and politics as well as ethics and morality, the Scottish thinker Adam Smith argued that, by looking after their own interests, people unintentionally served the needs of society as a whole.

Immanuel Kant

1724–1804

Arguably the most influential philosopher since Aristotle, Kant's achievements were immeasurable. His thinking in metaphysics, epistemology, ethics and aesthetics has influenced almost every philosophical movement that followed him right up to the present day.

BIOGRAPHY

Name Immanuel Kant

Born 1724

Place Königsberg, now Kaliningrad, Russia

Nationality German

Key facts Kant pioneered a new way of thinking, that the existence of knowledge presupposes the active participation of the human mind.

Died 1804

KEY WORKS

• *Critique of Pure Reason*

• *Critique of Practical Reason*

• *Prolegomena to Any Future Metaphysics*

New thinking for a new age

After financial difficulties forced him to give up his university studies Kant become a private tutor. Later on in life he finished his degree, became a lecturer and finally a professor. At around the same time he began to develop the ideas that were to make him famous and change the face of philosophy for ever.

Kant's thinking is notoriously difficult to comprehend fully, perhaps because, as well as devising a revolutionary new way of thinking he was at the same time inventing a new language with which to express his thoughts. Broadly speaking, his philosophy revolves around the proposition that the existence of knowledge presupposes the active participation of the human mind. He tried to demonstrate that the laws of nature and those of morality are both grounded in human reason. 'Two things fill the mind with ever-increasing wonder and awe,' he wrote, 'the starry heavens above me and the moral law within me.'

Achieving a synthesis

Kant's greatest treatise is undoubtedly his *Critique of Pure Reason*, which, after years of work, he finally published in 1781. It is a masterly synthesis of rationalism and empiricism, both of which put forward a one-sided view of knowledge. The rationalists claimed that metaphysical judgements – the essential fundamentals upon which all human knowledge is based – were established and justified purely by the intellect. The empiricists, on the other hand, held that the mind is a blank slate and that knowledge could be gained only through sensory experience.

Kant managed to reconcile these conflicting viewpoints in what he claimed was nothing less than philosophy's 'Copernican Revolution'. Rather than being a blank slate or piece of paper, he maintained that the mind plays an active part in shaping the world of experience. It imposes principles on experience, organizing and categorizing the sense data with which it is bombarded to generate knowledge.

As well as space and time, there were 12 fundamental categories according to Kant: substance, cause and effect, reciprocity, necessity, possibility, existence, totality, unity, plurality, limitation, reality and negation, which he christened 'forms of intuition'.

The 'categorical imperative'

In his first treatise, Kant claimed to have laid down new laws of thought by which he had determined the limits and the correct use of reason. In his second, the *Critique of Practical Reason*, he tackled the question of ethics, starting with the argument that it was reason alone that determined what was morally right and wrong. There was a universal moral law, which everyone should respect and obey, which he called the 'categorical imperative'.

Moral law, Kant argued, could not be hypothetical; it must be categorical. 'Act only on that maxim whereby you can at the same time will that it should be a universal law,' he wrote. It had to be consistent and applicable to everyone equally. Just as importantly, it was always necessary to consider the consequences of one's actions. 'Act in such a way that you always treat humanity, whether in yourself or in another, never simply as a means, but always at the same time as an end,' he counselled.

RIGHT: **Kant claimed to have discovered universal principles of thought that would be valid in perpetuity. He argued that knowledge could be gained only through a synthesis of experience and understanding.**

Edmund Burke

1729–1797

One of the foremost political thinkers of his day, Burke savagely attacked the Enlightenment philosophers who were 'so taken up with their theories about the rights of man, that they have totally forgot his nature'. Many consider him to be the father of modern conservatism.

BIOGRAPHY

Name Edmund Burke

Born 1729

Place Dublin

Nationality Anglo-Irish

Key facts Burke believed that society should not be tinkered with; it could change only organically, developing and adapting by itself in response to need.

Died 1797

KEY WORKS

• *A Philosophical Enquiry into the Origins of Our Ideas of the Sublime and Beautiful*

• *Reflections on the Revolution in France*

Settled principles

Educated at Trinity College, Dublin, as a lawyer (although he never practised law), Burke worked as an author and journalist before entering the House of Commons at the age of 37. He rapidly became a leading figure in the Whig Party and one of the most influential politicians of the day.

Although he supported the American colonists in their revolt against George III's government, he later became an arch-conservative. Throughout his long career he remained faithful to the philosophical principles that he had started to formulate while still an undergraduate. 'I have endeavoured all my life,' he wrote, 'to train my understanding and my temper in the studies and habits of philosophy,' concluding that 'my principles are all settled and arranged'.

Suspicion of the abstract

Burke's political philosophy had several strands. Chief among them was his suspicion of abstract ideas, especially when he suspected that they were agents for change. Abstract rights, for instance, were nothing more than 'a mine that will blow up at one grand explosion all examples of certainty'. This was why he despised Jean-Jacques Rousseau and the other thinkers of the French Enlightenment. They, he sneered, were putting forward 'a scheme of politics not adapted to the world in which they live'; they were 'so taken up with their theories about the rights of man that they have totally forgotten his nature'. Burke believed that, by definition, all human beings were imperfect. People, for him, were naturally a mixture of good and bad, and any notion that any human society could be perfect was pure fantasy.

> **❛** *In a democracy, the majority of the citizens is capable of exercising the most cruel oppression upon the minority.* **❜**

Revering the past

Burke found Enlightenment thinking repellent and alienating. He prided himself on being 'influenced by inborn feelings of nature and not being illuminated by a single ray of this new-sprung modern light'. Long before the French Revolution, which he denounced trenchantly in his *Reflections on the Revolution in France*, he had already taken issue with another typical Enlightenment belief, that clarity was an essential quality of great art. Great art, he suggested, strives after the infinite, which, as it has no fixed boundaries, can never be precisely defined. That is why we are so much more capable of being moved by suggestion than by anything clear cut and distinct.

An organic society

The outbreak of the French Revolution inspired Burke to his greatest outpourings. He constructed a veritable rogues' gallery of revolutionary politicians and of the philosophers who had inspired them. Their thinking was not only incorrect, it was dangerous. What Burke believed was that society had developed so much that no man could possibly claim to understand it. Dismantling it completely, which was what he thought the French revolutionaries were intending to do, would lead to disaster.

Social change should be gradual and natural, and society should be allowed to adapt to changing circumstances of its own volition. The view was extremely popular when Burke expressed it, and it has remained so among conservative thinkers ever since.

ABOVE: **Though he supported the grievances of the American colonists against the British crown, Burke was at heart a natural conservative and was quick to condemn the French Revolution for its bloody excesses.**

Thomas Paine

1737–1809

A radical propagandist who played a leading part in bringing about the American and French Revolutions, Paine argued that all men had an equal claim to political rights and that government must rest on the ultimate sovereignty of the people.

BELOW: **A key campaigner in the struggle for American independence, Paine argued that everyone, regardless of rank, was born with the same right, which could be protected only in a republican democracy.**

An extreme radical

Thomas Paine is a conundrum. It is unquestionable that he played a large part in inspiring the revolutions that gave birth to the USA and brought about the fall of the French monarchy. In his thinking, he anticipated modern views on human rights, atheism and rationalism. Yet, if it had not been for a lucky encounter with Benjamin Franklin, it is likely that Paine's philosophical career would have been stillborn. Franklin advised him to emigrate to America, where he emerged as a potent propagandist for American independence.

After the war Paine returned to England, where he wrote his most celebrated work, *The Rights of Man*. Charged with treason, he fled to France, where at first he was welcomed by the revolutionaries. Later, however, during the Reign of Terror the Jacobins had him arrested, and he escaped the guillotine only through the intervention of the American statesman James Monroe. Paine returned to America in 1802, where, old and ill, he spent the last years of his life in relative obscurity and poverty.

American revolutionary

In America Paine became editor of the *Pennsylvania Magazine*. He won immediate fame when he produced a pamphlet entitled *Common Sense*, which sold hundreds of thousands of copies. In it, Paine argued for immediate independence for the colonies, even if this meant war with Britain. The colonists, Paine said, had the right to create a society to be governed by democratically elected and accountable representatives. This government should be that of a republic, as Paine had no time for hereditary monarchy: 'Government by kings was the most prosperous invention the Devil ever set foot for the promotion of idolatry.'

Equal rights for all

Paine argued that monarchy and equality were incompatible. 'For all men being originally equal,' he wrote, 'no one by birth could have the right to set up his own family in perpetual preference to all others for ever.' He turned to the theme again in *The Rights of Man*, which he wrote after his return to England to defend the principles of the French Revolution against the savage attacks Edmund Burke had launched on them in *Reflections on the French Revolution*.

The will of the people

The Rights of Man is a seminal treatise on democracy and republicanism. Paine's view was that a government is legitimate only if it is established by the will of the people as a whole. Any government that denies this right is immoral and deserves to be overthrown. It was political dynamite.

After escaping death during the Reign of Terror, he returned to America, the land where he had first made his name. There, too, he found himself under attack. This was primarily because of the deist views he had expressed in his *The Age of Reason* – particularly his attacks on the Christian concept of a vengeful God and his belief that the Bible was the Word of God.

But, although he died poor and neglected, his thinking survived him to influence successive generations.

BIOGRAPHY

Name Thomas Paine

Born 1737

Place Thetford

Nationality English, later American

Key facts Paine's radical - for the day - views on democracy and religion influenced revolutionaries in France and America but eventually brought him into conflict with the societies he had helped create.

Died 1809

KEY WORKS

• *Common Sense*
• *The Rights of Man*
• *The Age of Reason*

Jeremy Bentham

1748–1832

Lawyer-turned-philosopher Jeremy Bentham was the leader of a group of 19th-century social-reforming British thinkers known as the Philosophical Radicals. He is best known as the founding father of a new ethical system, which he dubbed 'utilitarianism'.

Reformer and utilitarian

Bentham's moral philosophy revolved around what he called variously 'the greatest happiness principle' or 'the principle of utility'. He had a supremely practical mind, which was why the ethical system he devised started from a very simple principle: 'Nature,' he wrote, 'has placed mankind under the governance of two sovereign masters, pain and pleasure. It is for them alone to point out what we ought to do, as well as to determine what we shall do.'

The greatest happiness of the greatest number

The conclusion that Bentham drew from this was that people act

ABOVE: **Bentham believed in the principle of the greatest good for the greatest number of people.**

in order to maximize pleasure and minimize pain. He even devised what he termed a 'felicific calculus' to aid in the evaluation of how much of both qualities would result from any given action. Society's aim should be to promote 'the greatest happiness of the greatest number'. Utilitarianism had been born, and, although it has had its critics – notably those who say it does not allow for individual rights – for many it continues to have a substantial appeal.

Mary Wollstonecraft
1759–1797

An ardent campaigner for women's rights, Mary Wollstonecraft was the first feminist philosopher. Her revolutionary views on women, the church and the monarchy scandalized her contemporaries – one male critic described her as 'a hyena in petticoats'.

Early feminist

Following a decline in her family's fortunes Mary Wollstonecraft was forced to look for work, first as a lady's companion, then as a teacher and finally as a governess. However, through a chance introduction to the liberal publisher Joseph Johnson, she got the opportunity to write.

A Vindication of the Rights of Women

Published in 1792, *A Vindication of the Rights of Women* was her greatest book. It is a savage diatribe against the established social order.

Wollstonecraft called for better education for women as a right. Although she never spelled it out explicitly, her real demand was for women to be recognized as equals with men – 'Let woman share the rights and she will emulate the virtues of man' – advocating universal suffrage, the abolition of the monarchy and the disestablishment of the church.

Her contemporaries were shocked by the revolutionary nature of her views and scandalized by her private life. By the time she died in childbirth she had become largely marginalized, but in recent decades her reputation as a significant feminist thinker has become assured.

BIOGRAPHY

Name Mary Wollstonecraft

Born 1759

Place London

Nationality British

Key facts Radical, unconventional and flying in the face of disapproving society, Mary Wollstonecraft blazed a trail for women's rights at a time when much of what she espoused was unthinkable.

Died 1797

KEY WORKS

• *A Vindication of the Rights of Women*

LEFT:
Wollstonecraft's radical views included a call for the abolition of the monarchy.

The Modern Era

1800s–1950s In 19th-century Germany, philosophy entered a new golden age. Elsewhere, notably in Britain, philosophers championed political and social reform, while in the USA thinking became more pragmatic. In the succeeding century, faced with the challenges of modern science, philosophers began radically reassessing the nature of knowledge.

Arthur Schopenhauer, Johann Gottlieb Fichte and Friedrich Schelling started the German philosophical renaissance. They were later joined by Georg Hegel, who became Germany's dominant intellectual, and Karl Marx. The latter's ideas were to have more influence over a shorter time than those of any other thinker in history.

The early 20th century saw philosophy taking different directions. In Germany, Gottlob Frege redefined logic, while in Britain Bertrand Russell brought language to the forefront of the philosophical stage. Ludwig Wittgenstein devised two philosophical systems and became one of the most important thinkers of the century. Others, notably the existentialist Martin Heidegger, struggled to discover the meaning of life.

Johann Gottlieb Fichte

1762–1814

A disciple of Immanuel Kant, Fichte developed his own brand of idealistic philosophy, which he christened Wissenschaftslehre *(doctrine of scientific knowledge). He held that the empirical world is the creation of the knowing mind and that morality is the ultimate reality.*

BIOGRAPHY

Name Johann Gottlieb Fichte

Born 1762

Place Rammenau

Nationality German

Key facts Fichte held that the mind was the mainspring of the world and that reason reigned supreme. In his notion of 'logical necessity', he argued that seemingly empirical observations were deductible from scientific laws.

Died 1814

Controversial and contentious

Born into a poor family, Fichte won the patronage of a local notable who paid for his education. He worked as a private tutor while constructing the basis for his new philosophical theories and was later invited to become Professor of Critical Philosophy at the University of Jena. He remained there for four years until critical attacks – he was suspected of sympathy with atheism – forced him to quit. He once again became a tutor, this time in Berlin, where he remained for most of the rest of his life, eventually becoming head of the philosophy faculty and then rector of the city's newly founded university.

Fichte began his philosophical career as a disciple of Kant. His early reasoning so closely resembled Kant's thinking that when the *Critique of All Revelation* was first published anonymously many took it to have been written by Kant himself. Yet the two drifted apart. Kant took against Fichte on the one occasion they met and later condemned him for mistakenly having attempted to infer philosophical knowledge by the use of logic alone.

KEY WORKS

- *Critique of All Revelation*
- *The Science of Rights*
- *The Science of Ethics as Based on the Science of Knowledge*
- *The Vocation of Man, The Way Towards the Blessed Life*

❛ By philosophy the mind of man comes to itself and from henceforth rests on itself without foreign aid and is completely master of itself as the dancer of his feet, or the boxer of his hands. ❜

Fichte struck out on his own. Despite Kant's condemnation he became very popular, giving public lectures to packed houses and producing popular versions of his work to appeal to a wider audience. He constantly revised his philosophical system to make it clearer and more comprehensible, but many people found his philosophy hard to understand.

The 'pure I'

Fichte believed in what he termed 'logical necessity'. He argued that empirical observations could be deduced from scientific laws, adding that all philosophy must start from a single first principle. This, he said, could not be determined empirically. Rather it was simply known. It was also self-positing. Philosophers are still debating exactly what Fichte meant precisely by this. It seems to be bound up with the subjective self – what Fichte referred to as 'the pure I'. It is this 'I' that creates the empirical world of potential knowledge that is the foundation of all possible experience. It was upon this precept that Fichte built up an elaborate philosophical system, embracing the philosophy of science, nature, ethics, law and religion. It was intensely moral in its character, for Fichte believed that morality was the basis of all reality.

ABOVE: **An absolute idealist, Fichte believed that morality was the ultimate reality and that, as we were all moral beings, the moral will underpinned all human existence.**

A German nationalist

Not everyone accepted Fichte's reasoning, and he became more popular for his advocacy of German nationalism than as a pure philosopher. In 1813 he closed the University of Berlin so that its students could enlist in the Prussian army to fight Napoleon, while he himself volunteered to join the militia.

The next year, he was dead, having contracted typhus from his wife, who had caught it while nursing wounded soldiers in a military hospital. Whether he would have refined his philosophy still further, no one can say for certain. What can be said is that he was never satisfied with it. His career was a relentless striving for philosophical truth.

Georg Wilhelm Friedrich Hegel

1770–1831

One of the great systematic thinkers of all time, Hegel believed in an Absolute Spirit, which he held was identical with reality. His aim was to develop an all-embracing system of philosophy through which past, present and future could be interpreted and understood.

From theology to philosophy

Hegel was educated as a theology student before turning to philosophy and taking up a post at the University of Jena. His first major work, *Phenomenology of Spirit*, made his reputation, although it cost him his friendship with fellow-philosopher Friedrich von Schelling, whom he had known since their student days. When the university was forced to close after Jena was captured by Napoleon's army, Hegel worked as a newspaper editor and teacher before returning to university life, first at Heidelberg and then Berlin, where he remained for the rest of his career.

A misunderstood genius

In his lifetime Hegel was considered to be a philosophical colossus. After his death, though, much of his thinking was misinterpreted and distorted. Some held that his celebrated maxim – 'Man owes his entire existence to the state' – marked him out as the intellectual grandfather of Fascism. Then there was Karl Marx, who stood Hegel's teaching on its head to help him to devise his own pseudo-scientific philosophical, political and economic theories.

The truth is somewhat different, although some of the problems people have had in understanding what Hegel actually meant could well be down to the impenetrability of his prose, which is often extremely difficult to follow. Like Schilling, Hegel believed that reality was an organic unity in an ongoing process of development. It was the philosopher's task to chart this development, analysing it rationally, demonstrating how it manifested itself in nature and in human history and showing the purpose to which it was directed.

The Absolute and dialectic

For Hegel, this was all bound up with the existence of the Absolute (or Absolute Spirit) and his notion of the *Geist*. The former is pure thought; the latter is the stuff of existence, the ultimate essence of being. History was really the search of the *Geist* for absolute knowledge; it is never static, and individuals have no power to direct or control it – they are enveloped in the *Zeitgeist*, the spirit of the time. Driven on by the *Geist*, history is always moving forward.

The logic governing this could be supplied by the exercise of what he called 'dialectic'. Hegelian dialectic starts with a proposition or thesis, which, initially, is taken to be true. Then, an equally logical antithesis is formulated. Faced with two incompatible ideas, a third position becomes apparent. This is the synthesis. This becomes a new thesis, for which another antithesis becomes apparent and another synthesis generated. The process continues until the *Geist* recognizes itself as the ultimate reality. Hegel applied the same dialectic to his analysis of society and the role of the state. Here, he said, the process would come to an end only when the ideal of a conflict-free society was achieved.

Despite the fact that some of his thinking has come under subsequent attack, Hegel's place as one of philosophy's giants is secure.

ABOVE: **Hegel believed that, rather than being static, reality was a constant forward-moving process and the ultimate human goal was the achievement of self-recognition.**

James Mill
1773–1836

Although Mill's reputation now rests more on his collaboration with Jeremy Bentham in formulating the principles of utilitarianism than on his own philosophy, he was a formidable political thinker in his own right.

Social reformer

Following a meeting with Jeremy Bentham in 1807, Mill and Bentham became friends and political and philosophical partners, united in their call for social reform. Although they were to quarrel later, they laid down the principles of utilitarianism.

Essay on Government

Mill wrote five books and more than a thousand essays and reviews during his working life, but it is on one work – *Essay on Government* – that his reputation as a political theorist largely rests. It was intended, Mill wrote, to be a 'skeleton map' of politics.

The purpose of government for Mill was to maximize the happiness of the community as a whole. This could not be achieved by monarchy, aristocracy or even direct democracy. The answer was a representative democracy, in which citizens elect representatives to legislate on their behalf. Representative government, Mill said, was the 'grand discovery of modern times'. What he was really advocating, however, was not a democracy as we understand it, but a meritocracy, with the vote being given only to men aged over 40 and governed by men of what he called the 'middle rank', those we would now call middle class.

RIGHT: **Mill said that representative democracy was essential for 'the greatest good for the greatest number'.**

Arthur Schopenhauer

1788–1850

One of the first philosophers to declare that he was an atheist, Schopenhauer contended that the universe was not a rational place. He was the first great Western thinker to study Vedic and Buddhist philosophy seriously.

A natural pessimist

Born into a wealthy family, Schopenhauer never needed to work. Instead, he devoted his life to private study. For much of his life he was a disappointed man, and it was not until he reached the age of 63 that he finally enjoyed the critical success he craved. Not surprisingly, his thinking is on the whole pessimistic, revolving around the concept of what he termed the 'will'.

The will

Schopenhauer held the will to be an irrational universal force with no particular goal or object. The phenomenal world, he proclaimed, was without meaning or purpose. In fact, it was close to being an illusion. As for humanity, it was in a sorry state. We are nothing more than slaves to our desires as the will drives us inexorably onwards.

He did detect some saving graces, however. First, there was compassion, which Schopenhauer said was the true basis of ethics and also of love. Second, there were the arts, which could provide a momentary release from the torture of human existence. Many later philosophers, most notably Friedrich Nietzsche, Ludwig Wittgenstein and Karl Popper, were all influenced by his work.

LEFT: **Schopenhauer argued that the natural world was a savage place in which people had little to look forward to other than violence, injustice and death.**

103

Alexis de Tocqueville

1805–1859

A French aristocrat who became a noted political theorist, Alexis de Tocqueville pioneered a scientific approach to the study of human society. His aim, he said, was to create 'a new political science for a world quite new'.

Practical and theoretical

De Tocqueville combined a political career with his work as a political theorist. In *Democracy in America* he combined political science with sociological analysis to produce an in-depth view of his subject. The book has long been regarded as a pioneering classic, as has his *The Old Regime and the Revolution*.

As a political thinker, the way in which he analysed his subjects broke away from the methods by which his contemporaries thought society should be studied. For de Tocqueville, freedom was paramount. It was, he wrote, a 'sacred thing'. Bound up with this was his belief that people could be virtuous only if they were free and equal, and this equality could be found only in democracy. When he visited the USA he noted how he 'looked for an image of democracy itself, its penchants, its character and its passions'.

Democracy in America

Democracy in America is a compelling record of what de Tocqueville found. His description of a democratic society in action enabled him to identify the fundamental forces driving it and to establish how they affected every aspect of political and social life. The result is amazingly insightful. It has also stood the test of time, which is why de Tocqueville is still required reading for students of political philosophy.

> **❝** *In other words, a democratic government is the only one in which those who vote for a tax can escape the obligation to pay it.* **❞**

John Stuart Mill
1806—1873

Probably the foremost thinker in the English-speaking world during the 19th century, Mill championed the causes of utilitarianism and personal liberty. He was also noted for his contributions to logic, the philosophy of science, metaphysics and epistemology.

Educated by his father

John Stuart Mill did not attend school or university. He was educated at home by his father, later joining him in working for the East India Company. Mill made his philosophical reputation with *A System of Logic*, which he published in 1843, but his real claims to fame are *On Liberty*, *The Subjection of Women* and his classic restatement of the principles of utilitarianism.

In *On Liberty* he took as his thesis the notion that 'the sole end for which mankind is warranted, individually or collectively, in interfering with the liberty of any of their number, is self-protection'. The book is a classic exposition of the case for individual freedom.

Sexual equality

The Subjection of Women was also remarkable. His aim, he wrote, was to show 'that the principles which regulate the existing sexual relationships between the two sexes – the legal subordination of one sex to another – is wrong in itself and is now one of the chief hindrances to human improvement'. With statements like this, Mill became the first great thinker to state the case for sexual equality, even arguing in Parliament for women to be given the right to vote.

LEFT: **The champion of utilitarianism, John Stuart Mill was an ardent Victorian reformer who passionately defended the rights of individuals.**

Soren Kierkegaard

1813–1855

Generally recognized as the founding father of existentialism, Kierkegaard made his name initially through his trenchant criticism of Hegel. He himself believed that no system of thought could explain the unique experience of the individual satisfactorily.

BIOGRAPHY

Name Soren Kierkegaard

Born 1813

Place Copenhagen

Nationality Danish

Key facts Kierkegaard's philosophical writings were not understood during his lifetime. For him, what was most important in life was the individual's relationship with God.

Died 1855

KEY WORKS

• *Either/Or*

• *Fear and Trembling*

• *The Concept of Anxiety*

• *Concluding Unscientific Postscript*

Unhappy and misunderstood

Kierkegaard was born into a prosperous family, but his relatively short life – he died at the age of only 42 – was not a happy one. Like his father, he suffered from perpetual feelings of guilt and dread. He pessimistically forecast that his work would not be accepted while he was alive and that it would be only in the 20th century that the significance of his philosophical writings would be understood.

Kierkegaard was a philosophical outsider. He began his career by publishing a masterly criticism of the philosophy of Hegel and went on from this to reassert the importance of the individual and the problems of decision making. Philosophers, he believed, should concentrate on these rather than focusing wrongly on grand metaphysical schemes: 'The thing is to find a truth that is true for men, to find the idea for which I can live or die.'

Such thinking ran counter to the prevailing philosophical spirit of his times, which may be one reason why he decided to publish his philosophical works under pseudonyms, reserving his real name for his religious writings.

The three modes

There were, said Kierkegaard, three possible modes of existence. The first was aesthetic, which concerned the pursuit of pleasure and the quest for immediate gratification. The second was ethical, which was based on the principles of responsibility, obligation and duty. The third was religious.

This third mode caused Kierkegaard problems, since he could see how, all too easily, it could come into conflict with ethics. In *Fear and Trembling* he used the biblical story of Abraham and Isaac to highlight the conflict between the two. In response to God's order, Abraham is willing to sacrifice his only son. His religious commitment, said Kierkegaard, obliged him to act, or prepare to act, in a way that went completely against the accepted norms of moral behaviour. Abraham, Kierkegaard maintained, had been forced to put aside ethics for the sake of a higher *telos* (purpose) at the behest of God, who, as Kierkegaard pointed out, is actually the source of all moral law. Abraham was a true 'knight of faith', who sincerely believed that his son would be restored to him by God.

A question of faith

According to Kierkegaard, what mattered more than anything else in life was the relationship of the individual soul with God. Thus, it was only through his third mode of existence that humanity might find freedom and fulfilment. It required a 'leap of faith', a step in the dark taken with 'fear and trembling'. 'Faith', Kierkegaard wrote, 'is the greatest passion in a human being. What our age lacks is not reflection but passion. The conclusions of passion are the only reliable ones.'

Faith was irrational. It had to be taken on trust, as reason can only undermine faith and never justify it. For Kierkegaard there was no point in trying to devise a rational proof for the existence of God. Either we choose to believe in God or we do not. If we do, the commitment must be total. We must believe wholeheartedly and passionately, for both God and Christianity are necessarily beyond any rational analysis or understanding.

Karl Marx

1818–1883

Without doubt, Marx was the most influential political thinker the Victorian age produced. It is impossible to understand the history of the 20th century without reference to his philosophy. His revolutionary ideas literally changed the world.

BIOGRAPHY

Name Karl Marx

Born 1818

Place Trier

Nationality German

Key facts Marx predicted that the seizing of the means of production by the proletariat would be the inevitable consequence of capitalism, replacing the capitalist 'epoch' with a fairer, classless society.

Died 1883

KEY WORKS

- *The Communist Manifesto* (with Engels)
- *Das Kapital*

An extreme radical

Marx studied at the universities of Bonn and Berlin, but his Jewish background, radical political stance and militant atheism made it impossible for him to secure an academic post once he had graduated. Instead, he turned to journalism, where his trenchantly expressed views led to the newspaper he edited being shut down. He moved to Paris, where he met Friedrich Engels, the son of a wealthy cotton manufacturer who had been sent to manage the family factories in Britain. The two became lifelong friends and intellectual collaborators. They wrote *The Communist Manifesto* together, and Engels helped the poverty-stricken Marx out financially over the years. Marx finally settled in London, where he lived for the rest of his life.

Marx was a confident political theorist. His world view was comprehensive and revolutionary. Drawing on his knowledge of history and economics as well as philosophy, he set about constructing a philosophical system based firmly on what later was to be christened 'dialectical materialism'. The result was something unique. What Marx concluded was that historical, political and economic developments of the kind he was outlining were inevitable. His theories, he claimed, were totally scientific. They enabled him to predict the future development of society with pinpoint accuracy. Capitalism, he stated confidently, would inevitably collapse to be replaced by a new classless society, a Communist one.

Employing dialectic

Marx borrowed many of his philosophical ideas – notably the notion of the dialectic – from Hegel, but he gave them a twist that stood Hegel's thinking completely on its head. Unlike Hegel, he was not an idealist, but a self-proclaimed materialist. 'The philosophers,' Marx proclaimed, 'have only interpreted the world in various ways. The point is to change it.'

> *What the bourgeoisie produces… is its own gravediggers. Its fall and the victory of the proletariat are equally inevitable… The proletarians have nothing to lose but their chains.*

Marx used the dialectic, the lessons he drew from history and his views on economics to indicate how this change would come about. In his view, society passed through various 'epochs', each characterized by its particular economic structure. Thanks in large part to the Industrial Revolution, he and his fellow Victorians were living in the capitalist age.

Prophet of revolution

Marx went on to predict that developments in industrial technology would inevitably throw more and more ordinary people out of work. The workers would become more and more impoverished, while the capitalists – the owners and controllers of the means of production – would grow richer and richer. Eventually the workers would unite, rise up against the capitalists, overthrow them and take the means of production into their own hands. Capitalism, therefore, was riddled with economic contradictions and ever-increasing social tensions that would bring about its downfall: 'Its fall and the victory of the proletariat are equally inevitable.'

Marx's thinking had tremendous appeal. It was also wrong on a number of levels. He predicted that the revolution would break out in Germany first. It did not. He said that the triumph of the workers would lead to a classless society and, eventually, the 'withering away' of the state. It did not. This was why subsequent Marxist thinkers – notably Lenin – qualified Marx's dogmas to explain why, although worldwide revolution was still inevitable, it would not happen in the way he had presupposed.

Friedrich Engels

1820–1895

Friend of and collaborator with Karl Marx, Engels was the joint father of Communism. His principal philosophical contribution to Marxism was to develop the doctrine of 'dialectical materialism'.

A wealthy revolutionary

Engels came from a wealthy family of textile manufacturers. He and his father did not get on, so he dropped out of school and became a clerk. It was then that he began reading the philosophy of Hegel, which changed his life. The other catalyst was his meeting with Marx, although, even before this, Engel had developed profoundly radical views. The two men collaborated on *The Communist Manifesto*; after Marx's death, Engels edited *Das Kapital*, Marx's unfinished masterpiece. This did not stop him from working on his own writings, the most important of which was *The Origin of the Family, Private Property and the State*.

Engels spent much of his life juggling two extraordinarily contrasting personalities. On the one hand, there was the frock-coated, plutocratic Manchester mill-owner who spent his leisure time hunting with the Cheshire Hounds and his evenings immersed in the study of military history. On the other, there was the romantic radical, who, together with his friend Karl Marx, preached socialist revolution and was the effective co-father of Communism.

> *All history has been a history of class struggles between dominant classes at various stages of social development.*

BIOGRAPHY

Name Friedrich Engels

Born 1820

Place Barmen

Nationality German

Key facts Although he came from a wealthy mill-owning family, Engels, together with Karl Marx, was responsible for some of the most radical political theorizing of recent times.

Died 1895

Although some of his political friends found these two extremes incompatible, Engels himself was not concerned. On hearing that he was being accused of hypocrisy, he wrote laconically to Marx that he did not 'give a damn'. He saw no reason why a fondness for good champagne should not go hand-in-hand with devotion to the socialist cause.

'Workers of the world, unite'

Long before he met Marx, Engels had been converted to radicalism. His beliefs were coloured by his experiences in Manchester, which, thanks to the Industrial Revolution and the cotton industry, was the most prosperous city in the country. In *The Condition of the Working Class in England* he wrote scathingly of the 'refuse, offal and sickening filth' of the city and savagely denounced the effects this had on the workers in its factories and mills: 'Women are made unfit for childbearing, children deformed, men enfeebled, limbs crushed, whole generations wrecked, afflicted with disease and infirmity purely to fill the purses of the bourgeoisie.'

What was true of Manchester was true of all other great cities and towns: 'Everywhere', he wrote, 'there is barbarous indifference, hard egoism on the one hand and nameless misery on the other.' Social conditions were so appalling that it was amazing 'the whole crazy fabric' still hung together. There could be only one outcome: socialism. The dialectic confirmed Engels in his views.

KEY WORKS

• *The Condition of the Working Class in England*

• *The Communist Manifesto* (with Marx)

• *The Origin of the Family, Private Property and the State*

A lifelong revolutionary

This was Engels in 1844, relatively early on his career as a political thinker. Four decades later he was still on the attack, this time targeting the institution of the family. Families, he said, were unnatural. They were spawned by capitalism and designed to privatize wealth and human relationships in a way that contradicted the natural course of evolution. Class, the inequality between the sexes and private property all came under his lash.

Engel's legacy was potent, and there is no doubt that he and Marx were responsible for some of the most explosive turns in 20th-century history.

LEFT: **Together with Marx, Engels laid the foundations of Communism, calling for the workers of the world to unite and overthrow the capitalist system.**

Henry Sidgwick

1838–1900

The single most influential ethical philosopher of the Victorian era, Henry Sidgwick spent his entire career teaching at the University of Cambridge. The Methods of Ethics, which he wrote in the 1880s, is generally considered to be one of the classics of moral philosophy.

BIOGRAPHY

Name Henry Sidgwick

Born 1838

Place Skipton

Nationality British

Key facts Having entered Trinity College, Cambridge, as an undergraduate, Sidgwick never left the university. He became Professor of Moral Philosophy in 1885, holding the post until his death.

Died 1900

KEY WORKS

• *The Methods of Ethics*

Making ethics relevant

Sidgwick was a utilitarian, a disciple of Jeremy Bentham and John Stuart Mill. He was also a considerable philosopher in his own right. In *The Methods of Ethics* he set out his aims right at the start. They were to define the 'methods of ethics' implicit in everyday moral reasoning and to find if it was possible to discover a rational and, at the same time, principled basis for deciding how one ought to act.

Ethical choices

According to Sidgwick, the choice was between egoism, intuitionism and utilitarianism. He concluded that what he defined as the 'morality of common sense' was, to some extent, 'unconsciously utilitarian'. He also demonstrated how utilitarianism could be reconciled with intuitionism and the two integrated into a single ethical system. What Sidgwick had problems with, however, was the relationship between utilitarianism and egoism. Although the reasons for both were valid, he found that they were ultimately irreconcilable.

ABOVE: **In his speculations on ethics, Sidgwick tried to reconcile the conflicting principles of egoism and utilitarianism.**

Sidgwick's thinking has had a lasting influence. Later thinkers – notably Bertrand Russell and Peter Singer – have all acknowledged him as an important contributor to their philosophical thought.

Charles Sanders Pierce

1839–1914

The founder of American pragmatism – he renamed it 'pragmaticism' to avoid confusion – Charles Pierce was a scientist who took up philosophy as a hobby. He was an apostle of the scientific method, which he believed was the best way of overcoming philosophical doubt.

A scientist first

During his lifetime, Pierce was better known as a scientist than as a philosopher. He taught mathematics at John Hopkins University and, for many years, worked for the US Coast and Geodetic Survey. After he was forced to leave government employment as a result of a financial scandal in which he was later shown not to have been involved, he spent the rest of his life in poverty.

Defining 'pragmaticism'

The guiding principle on which Pierce based all his reasoning was as follows: 'If one can define accurately all the conceivable experimental phenomena which the affirmation or denial of a concept could imply, one will have a complete definition of the concept.'

Pierce went further. Only by establishing a consensus of opinion, he argued, can we hope to arrive at philosophical truth. This – and indeed reality – is therefore whatever the consensus opinion says it is.

RIGHT: **Though neglected in his lifetime, Pierce is now recognized as the true father of American pragmatism. He believed logic to be the essential basis of all philosophical speculation.**

BIOGRAPHY

Name Charles Sanders Pierce

Born 1839

Place Cambridge, Massachusetts

Nationality American

Key facts A man of science first and a philosopher second, Pierce dubbed his pragmaticism the 'philosophy of the laboratory scientist'.

Died 1914

KEY WORKS

• *The Essential Pierce*

William James

1842–1910

Psychologist and philosopher William James was the leading exponent of American pragmatism. He believed that the mind is goal directed and that consciousness – what he termed 'the stream of thought' – exists in a constant state of flux.

Philosopher and psychologist

James, along with Charles Sanders Pierce and John Dewey, was one of the founders of the first home-grown American philosophical system: pragmatism. There are several important underlying themes in James's philosophy, including religion, human responses to life, and the notion that we all help to 'create' the truths that we 'register'. To a great extent, his philosophy is bound up with his understanding of psychology. Indeed, he concentrated on the latter before eventually turning to pure philosophical speculation.

Probing mind and thought

The Principles of Psychology, James's first major work, was an in-depth analysis of the mind and the relationship between it, consciousness and thought. The latter, he argued, had developed as part of the evolutionary process, while consciousness was best defined as a 'stream of thought'. The book took James 12 years to write and, when he finally finished it, he was deeply dissatisfied with the end result – in a letter to his publisher Henry Holt, he described it as 'a loathsome, distended, bloated dropsical mass'. He never wrote about psychology again, and he spent the rest of his life developing and expanding his purely philosophical ideas. What he concentrated on was advancing the concept of pragmatism, which had been originally articulated by his friend Charles Sanders Pierce.

The difference between the two men's approach was simple: Pierce had advocated pragmatism as a theory of meaning; James, on the other hand, postulated that it was a theory of truth. By definition, all knowledge must be pragmatic, therefore, by applying the principles of pragmatic reasoning, it was possible to determine which parts of it were true. If, he said, we 'grant an idea or belief to be true', the questions that must be asked are: 'What concrete difference will its being true make to anyone's actual life? How will the truth be realized? What experiences will be different from those which would obtain if the belief were false? What, in short, is the truth's cash value in experiential terms?'

The practical pragmatist

What James was saying was that, if a statement could not be disproved, people were justified in believing in it if they benefited from it. He used the argument to justify belief in the existence of God. Religious belief, he said, involved taking a stand. There was no middle ground. The choice to believe or not to believe in God was thus what he termed a 'forced' issue. It was also a 'momentous' one. James argued that it was preferable to be a believer, since, according to pragmatic principles, people's lives are made better by such a belief.

Although James had his critics – notably those who considered his arguments for belief in God simplistic – his overall thinking proved extremely influential. Bertrand Russell and Ludwig Wittgenstein both learned from him, while, more recently, the work of such neopragmatist philosophers as Richard Rorty demonstrates clearly the permanence of James's influence and ideas.

Friedrich Nietzsche

1844–1900

The controversial German philosopher Friedrich Nietzsche challenged Christianity and its moral code, which he held was life denying. He argued that the time had come to replace this outdated religion with a more positive, life-affirming alternative.

Anarchic genius

The son of a Protestant pastor, Nietzsche came to reject his Christian upbringing. A gifted scholar – he became a professor at Basel University at the age of only 24 – he never studied philosophy formally. He turned to it after reading Schopenhauer, building on what he found there to develop a philosophical system of his own. Eventually, he turned against Schopenhauer's teachings, arguing that the pessimism that dominated them was unfounded. To get the most out of life, it had to be lived to the full in accordance with a new life-affirming system. While still only in his forties, Nietzsche went mad, and he died insane.

Nietzsche is one of the most misunderstood philosophers of all time. He was not a prophet of Fascism and Nazism, as many subsequent thinkers have stated. He scorned German nationalism and was contemptuous of anti-Semitism in all its guises. Nor was he a nihilist. His philosophical thought is demonstrably independent and unique.

Nietzsche tackled a wide range of topics, from morals, ethics and religion to metaphysics and epistemology. Uniting all of them was one central doctrine. He called it the 'will to power', which, he claimed, was the inevitable consequence of the evolutionary process. People needed to learn how to sublimate and control their natural passions and turn the 'will to power' into a creative force, making them masters of their own destinies, the supermen of Nietzsche's dreams.

'God is dead'

Achieving this meant doing away with such outdated ideas as the 'slave morality' that he believed characterized Christianity. He had little time for the greatest thinkers of the past, famously dismissing Socrates as 'degenerate'. As for God, he wrote that 'we philosophers and "free spirits" feel ourselves irradiated as by a new dawn by the report that the "old God is dead"'. Traditional philosophy and religion were positively

harmful in their effects, enervating and degrading the natural capacity for achievement that all human beings possessed. Something new was needed, something that would lead to a new kind of freedom for humanity: 'At last the horizon seems open once more, granting even that it is not bright; our ships can at last put out to sea in face of every danger; every hazard is again permitted to the discerner; the sea, our sea, again lies open before us; perhaps never before did such an "open sea" exist.'

The process, Nietzsche recognized, would not be an easy one, but the superman, when he emerged, would be the modern-day equivalent of Aristotle's man of virtue. The 'lightning out of the dark cloud of man', he would fulfil the supreme aim of 'becoming what one is'. He was the man of the future, the man of destiny. Nietzsche's thinking set the agenda for many subsequent thinkers – both for him and against – in the 20th century.

ABOVE: **Nietzsche argued that people should not be expected to follow the examples of societies that no longer existed and religions in which fewer and fewer people believed.**

Gottlob Frege

1848–1925

Although his work went largely unnoticed in his lifetime, Frege is today accepted as one of the giants of contemporary philosophy. He devised a revolutionary system of mathematical logic that overthrew Aristotle's reasoning and laid the foundations for modern analytical thought.

BIOGRAPHY

Name Gottlob Frege

Born 1848

Place Wismar

Nationality German

Key facts Possibly the greatest logician who ever lived, Frege attempted to demonstrate that all basic arithmetical truths could be deduced from purely logical axioms.

Died 1925

KEY WORKS

- *Conceptual Notation*
- *The Foundations of Arithmetic*
- *On Sense and Reference*

Father of modern logic

A mathematician by training, Frege spent the whole of his academic career working in the mathematics department of the University of Jena, and his work remained largely ignored until Bertrand Russell discovered it fairly late in Frege's life. It was at Jena that he invented quantificational logic and made groundbreaking advances in the philosophy of mathematics and that of language – his interest in logic grew out of his interest in the foundations of arithmetic.

Frege may well merit the title of the greatest logician who has ever lived. When he rejected Aristotle's classic method of analysing a sentence by splitting it into subject and predicate and, instead, substituted a mathematical method of analysis based on function and argument, he set in train a philosophical revolution that was to have profound consequences for the subject as a whole.

Frege called this new logical language *Begriffsschrift*, which roughly translates as 'concept notation'. The concept is fairly simple to understand. For example, if the sentence 'Plato is wise' is analysed the Aristotelian way, 'Plato' is obviously the subject of the sentence and 'is wise' is the property ascribed to the subject. In Frege's view, far from being logical, Aristotle's approach was illogical and incorrect. Employing his new logic, the same sentence contains a function 'X is wise'; 'Plato' is the argument, filling the gap in what otherwise would be an incomplete functional expression. The principle is the same as the one used in basic mathematics. 'There is nothing more objective,' he stated, 'than the laws of arithmetic.'

> *Just as 'beautiful' points the way for aesthetics and 'good' for ethics, so do words like 'true' for logic.*

Mathematics and language

Frege employed the same logical principles in his efforts to develop a philosophy of mathematics. Mathematical truths, he said, must be logical truths. But he did not stop there. When it came to language, his speculations proved equally influential. Neither a functional expression nor an argument could mean much – if anything – taken on their own; they only worked in the context of a sentence in terms of the contribution they make to the sense of the expression. Frege labelled these twin concepts the 'context principle' and 'the compositionality of meaning'. Both have proved to be of major philosophical significance, as has his basic precept that logical relationships were independent of human thought – in other words, they were objective truth.

According to Frege's arguments, this meant that, although ideas might vary from person to person, what he termed their *Sinn* (sense) could not. This meant that referring was not the sole linguistic function of proper names, they also possess an additional linguistic feature: their sense. Frege called this the 'theory of sense and reference'.

ABOVE: **Frege held that 'every good mathematician is at least half a philosopher and every good philosopher is at least half a mathematician'. He spent much of his career in obscurity until 1903, when Bertrand Russell drew attention to the importance of his work.**

Frege's legacy

The importance of Frege's contributions to philosophy is incalculable. His work deeply influenced not only Bertrand Russell but also many other philosophers, including Rudolf Carnap, a leading exponent of logical positivism, and the young Ludwig Wittgenstein, although the latter was later to repudiate Frege's thinking. As far as the philosophy of language is concerned, it lies at the heart of the arguments put forward by those modern philosophers who are striving to demonstrate how language is linked to reality.

Émile Durkheim

1858–1917

Generally regarded as the founding father of sociology, Durkheim believed that society's social fabric was cemented together by a code of moral rules. In modern society, he argued, what he termed 'moral individualism' marked the birth of a new economic and social order.

BIOGRAPHY

Name Émile Durkheim

Born 1858

Place Épinal

Nationality French

Key facts Long recognized as a pivotal figure in the development of social scientific thought, Durkheim preferred to be described as a social philosopher rather than as a sociologist.

Died 1917

KEY WORKS

• *The Division of Labour in Society*

• *Rules of the Sociological Method*

• *Suicide*

A born academic

The son of a rabbi and a brilliant scholar, Durkheim was destined from the start for an academic career. After a spell as a teacher and further study in Germany, he was appointed to a post at the University of Bordeaux, where he wrote his first major works. Eventually he moved to Paris, becoming a professor at the Sorbonne, where he remained for the rest of his career. Durkheim's final years were unhappy. He never fully recovered from the death of his only son, who died in the early days of the First World War, and, after suffering a stroke, Durkheim died at the age of only 59.

'Having begun from philosophy,' he wrote, 'I tend to return to it; or rather I have been quite naturally drawn back to it by the nature of the questions which I met along my route.' Philosophically speaking, Durkheim could be classed as a positivist, even though he himself disliked the term. 'Our main objective', he wrote, 'is to extend to human conduct scientific rationalization by showing that, considered in the past, such conduct can be reduced to relations between cause and effect, and that an equally rational operation can subsequently transform into rules of action for the future.'

Learning from the past

What this involved was a thorough and scientific investigation of the moral rules that he held bound the fabric of all human societies together. This meant digging back into the past to learn from examples rather than indulging in theoretical speculation.

Durkheim argued that sociology, as he understood it, was based on a single fundamental principle: 'the objective reality of social facts'. By 'facts', he meant social phenomena, factors or causes; by saying that they should be studied as 'things', he meant that they were to be seen as

> ❝ *Man's privilege is that the bond he accepts is not physical but moral – that is, social. He is governed not by a material environment brutally imposed upon him, but by a conscience superior to his own, the superiority of which he feels. He escapes the body's yoke, but is subject to that of society.* ❞

'realities external to the individual and independent of any conceptual apparatus'. The 'facts' worked together much like the parts of a machine. They formed, he said, a continuum, mirroring society's gradual evolution.

BELOW: **Durkheim argued that society is cemented together by strict moral rules.**

'Moral individualism' and *anomie*

As a result of his researches, Durkheim concluded that, as societies evolve from a 'mechanical' to an 'organic' state, what he termed the 'collective consciousness' weakens. In an organic society the trend was towards individualism. 'In the same way as the ideal of less developed societies was to create as intense a shared life as possible in which the individual was absorbed,' he wrote, 'our ideal is constantly to introduce greater equality in our social relations in order to ensure the free unfolding of socially useful forces.'

What had to be avoided at all costs was a condition he described as '*anomie*'. In this state, moral norms become confused, unclear or are simply not present at all. In such a condition individuals find that there are no limits set on their desires, and their aspirations become infinite in scope. Durkheim said this was totally undesirable: 'To pursue a goal which by definition is unattainable is to condemn oneself to a state of perpetual unhappiness.'

Edmund Husserl

1858–1938

Edmund Husserl became one of the most influential philosophers of the 20th century. He believed that the philosophical discipline he pioneered, phenomenology, would provide a basis for all human knowledge and establish philosophy as a 'rigorous science'.

BIOGRAPHY

Name Edmund Husserl

Born 1858

Place Prossnitz, now Prostějov, Czech Republic

Nationality Austrian

Key facts Husserl pioneered phenomenology, a system based on the premise that reality consists of objects and events as perceived in human consciousness and not existing independently of it.

Died 1938

KEY WORKS

• *Logical Investigations*

• *Ideas*

• *Formal and Transcendental Logic*

Analysing experience

Although Jewish by birth, Husserl converted to Catholicism in 1887. However, this did not stop him being persecuted by the Nazis and effectively banned from German academic life in his final years. Educated in Leipzig, Berlin and Vienna, where he became a disciple of fellow philosopher and psychologist Franz Brentano, Husserl taught at the universities of Halle, Gottingen and Freiburg, gradually developing the philosophical system that was to bring him fame.

Husserl's new approach to philosophy was revolutionary. It was built around a systematic analysis of experience, carried out in a way that had never been attempted before. The name Husserl gave his philosophical system – phenomenology – comes from the fact that it treats everything as a phenomenon. 'The whole world, when one is in the phenomenological attitude,' he wrote, 'is not accepted as actuality, but only as actuality-phenomenon. I exist, and all that is not-I is mere phenomenon dissolving into phenomenal connections.'

Husserl borrowed the concept of intentionality – the idea that all conscious states relate to a content regardless of whether or not that content actually exists – from Franz Brentano, who had taught him in Vienna. However, his real starting point was Descartes, with whom he agreed that there is only one thing of which we can be absolutely certain: conscience awareness.

> *A new fundamental science, pure phenomenology, has developed within philosophy. This is a science of a thoroughly new type and endless scope.*

What Husserl did was to redefine this principle. People, he said, are never simply conscious; they are always conscious of something – a book, another person's presence or a headache, for example. It followed that consciousness could be defined as 'directedness towards an object'. Husserl went on to suggest that what we can be sure of is that, regardless of whether anything of which we are aware actually exists independently, it is an object of consciousness as far as we are concerned. It was on this premise that he based all that followed.

'Phenomenological reduction'

Husserl called this 'phenomenological reduction'. Objects were 'appearances' rather than things in themselves. The problem of whether they existed or not had to be put to one side – 'bracketing' was Husserl's word for it. Through this, he believed that he could gradually build up an immensely valuable classification of conscious states and the many varied ways in which they were directed towards objects.

Husserl reasoned that we should put our 'natural attitude' to objects on hold so that they can be considered purely as they appear to our consciousness. His believed that by focusing on pure experience it would be possible to probe the directedness of consciousness itself. He termed this approach 'transcendental idealism'.

A lasting influence

To his critics, Husserl's arguments appeared somewhat paradoxical. How, they asked, could be possibly reconcile his claim that consciousness constitutes the objects to which it is directed with the fact that the external world has a reality of its own?

Husserl never totally answered this question. Nevertheless, his speculations have proved immensely valuable, influencing other equally important thinkers, notably Martin Heidegger and Jean-Paul Sartre. His notion of the *Lebenswelt* (life-world) has impacted deeply on sociology, while, more recently, some analytical philosophers have also adopted some of his precepts and principles.

ABOVE: **After the First World War, Husserl held that what he termed 'the crisis of European existence' could be overcome. Europe, he said, would be reborn 'from the spirit of philosophy through the heroism of reason'.**

John Dewey

1859–1952

A leading exponent of philosophical naturalism, John Dewey became the doyen of American philosophy. As well as being an outstanding philosopher, he won fame as an educationalist – advocating that children should 'learn by doing' – and as a psychologist.

The people's philosopher

Dewey held posts at the universities of Michigan and Chicago before moving to Columbia University in New York, where he stayed for the rest of his career. A man of varied interests who believed that part of his mission was to communicate his ideas to a mass audience, he became a widely known and respected popular figure.

Having begun as a follower of Hegel, Dewey abandoned Hegelian idealism in favour of pragmatism soon after being appointed to the University of Chicago in the 1890s. Following in the footsteps of Charles Darwin, he believed that the natural world existed in a state of evolutionary flux, as its various constituents interacted with each other. Thought, he reasoned, had to be understood genetically, while knowledge controlled and guided the interaction, a process he called 'instrumentalism'.

LEFT: **Pragmatist philosopher, psychologist and noted educational reformer, Dewey became a major public figure, noted for his down-to-earth democratic views.**

Investigating knowledge

Dewey went on from this to devise his celebrated Theory of Inquiry, which lay at the heart of all his subsequent philosophical thinking. People, he believed, learn how to behave in fairly predictable ways. They possess habits. Sometimes, though, these habits break down in the face of novel or unexpected experiences. The precepts in his theory, Dewey claimed, would enable people to formulate ideas and beliefs, so allowing them to respond to new or changed situations appropriately.

The process demanded the use of reasoning, what Dewey termed 'intellection'. It also required creative imagination: 'It involves going beyond what is given in the situation; it involves a leap, a jump, the propriety of which cannot be absolutely warranted in advance, no matter what precautions be taken.'

There were various stages to the process. The first was the decision to act to resolve the situation, isolating the problematic elements and formulating them into a problem-solving equation. This was followed by the construction of a number of hypotheses and working through their implications.

Finally, there came what Dewey held to be the crucial part of the entire process, which he called 'testing', in which each hypothesis is evaluated against actual experience. 'If we look and find present all the conditions demanded by the theory, and if we find the characteristic traits called for by rival alternatives to be lacking, the tendency to believe, to accept, is almost irresistible.' For him, 'the truth is that which works'. If a hypothesis passed the test, it was a 'warranted assertion'.

Expanding the system

Dewey thought that what worked for knowledge would also work for ethics, education and social theory. Learning should not be didactic – he passionately believed that children learn more when they are encouraged to be imaginative. The educational process should begin with and build on the interests of the child.

When it came to morals and ethics, Dewey's position was equally clear. He believed that moral precepts were confirmable hypotheses and that value judgements were the tools that helped people lead better lives. What ultimately is ethically good was 'a unified orderly release in action' of all the conflicting tensions that arise as a result of moral conflicts. Like truth, good, for Dewey, is ultimately what works.

BIOGRAPHY

Name John Dewey

Born 1859

Place Burlington

Nationality American

Key facts One of the founders of the philosophy of pragmatism and of functional psychology, Dewey was also an influential progressive educationalist.

Died 1952

KEY WORKS

- *The School and Society*
- *How We Think*
- *Human Nature and Conduct*
- *Logic: The Theory of Inquiry*

Henri Louis Bergson

1859–1941

The most influential French philosopher of the early part of the 20th century, Henri Bergson won international fame through his assertion that what he called the 'élan vital' (life force) and matter are the two opposing realities that dominate the universe.

BIOGRAPHY

Name Henri Louis Bergson

Born 1859

Place Paris

Nationality French

Key facts Bergson argued that the intuition is deeper than the intellect – a challenge to the mechanistic, Darwinian view of nature.

Died 1941

KEY WORKS

- *Time and Free Will*
- *Matter and Memory*
- *Creative Evolution*
- *The Two Sources of Morality and Religion*

Identifying the life force

A brilliant classics and mathematics student, Bergson began to study philosophy in 1878. Three years later, he started his long teaching career, culminating in his appointment to a professorship at the Collège de France, Paris, where his lectures drew huge audiences. His most celebrated contribution to philosophy was the concept of the *élan vital* (life force). This, Bergson argued, was the creative force that shaped life and, rather than Darwinian natural selection, drove evolution. At the end of his life, he clashed with the Vichy regime in France. He was offered exemption from anti-Semitic legislation if he renounced his Jewish faith, but he refused to do so.

ABOVE: **Having started out as a teacher, Bergson emerged as a philosopher of renown.**

Two worlds

Like others among his French contemporaries, Bergson was not as interested in the specifics of science, logic and analysis as he was in far-reaching general speculations. He offered insights rather than

Alfred North Whitehead

1861–1947

A mathematician and a philosopher, Alfred North Whitehead was, with Bertrand Russell, co-author of Principia Mathematica. *Many believe that this is the greatest single contribution to the study of logic since Aristotle.*

Master of metaphysics

Whitehead began academic life as a mathematician and logician, teaching at Cambridge – where Bertrand Russell was among his pupils – and the University of London before becoming Professor of Philosophy at Harvard. It was there that he developed the comprehensive metaphysical system that is now known as 'process philosophy'.

He is probably best known for his so-called 'philosophy of organism', which rejected materialism for a system of thinking centred on 'the concepts of life, organism, function, instantaneous reality, interaction, and order of nature'. In some ways, it can be seen as an inversion of Kant: 'For Kant the world emerges from the subject; for the philosophy of organism, the subject emerges from the world.'

A new synthesis

What Whitehead was attempting to produce was a synthesis between metaphysics and science. For him, 'organism' mattered more than 'substance', and 'event' more than the fixed parameters of space and time. 'In a certain sense,' he commented, 'everything is everywhere at all times.' His ultimate aim was to explain the connection between objective, scientific and logical descriptions of the world and the more everyday world of subjective experience.

RIGHT: **Whitehead rejected traditional scientific materialism for what he termed the 'philosophy of organism'.**

George Santayana
1863–1952

A major figure in American philosophical thinking, Santayana was a pioneer of naturalism. As well as writing philosophy, he was a prolific poet – he held poetry to be 'an expressive celebration of life'.

BIOGRAPHY

Name George Santayana

Born 1863

Place Madrid

Nationality Spanish

Key facts Philosopher, essayist, novelist and poet, Santayana believed human cognition and culture evolved to harmonize with the conditions in their environment, and their usefulness should be judged by how much they add to human happiness.

Died 1952

KEY WORKS

- *The Sense of Beauty*
- *The Life of Reason*
- *Scepticism and Animal Faith*
- *The Realms of Being*

A sceptic who doubted ideals

Santayana studied philosophy at Harvard and Berlin. On returning to the USA he joined the Harvard philosophy department. In 1912 he inherited a substantial legacy, and he retired. Turning down other academic posts – although continuing to write – he spent the rest of his life in Europe, finally settling in Rome, where he died.

Philosophically speaking, Santayana was an anti-idealist. He was also something of a sceptic. 'Perhaps,' he wrote, 'there is no source of things at all, the simple form from which they are evolved, but only an endless succession of different complexities.' He argued that everything had a natural basis. There were, he said, four major 'realms of being': essence, matter, spirit and truth. Matter was 'the principle of existence'. Knowledge was a compound of conviction, animal faith and intuitive essence.

Santayana believed fervently that creative imagination was central to human endeavour, urging people to 'cultivate it, love it and give it endless forms'. This was the way to establish meanings and values, which were generated by the interaction of the individual psyche and the material environment in which we exist.

RIGHT: **Santayana was a naturalist, who believed that it was the philosopher's task to celebrate the things that make life worth living.**

Max Weber

1864–1920

Arguably the most influential social theorist of the 20th century, Weber had an enduring influence on the development of political and social thought. He was a founding father of what became known as 'modernity'.

Subjective sociology

Weber studied law at the universities of Heidelberg – where he later taught – and Berlin before turning to political economy and then to other branches of sociology. Following a nervous breakdown in 1896, he largely stopped teaching for over 20 years but continued to write, focusing in particular on world religions and economic and legal sociology.

He spearheaded a revolution in sociology, arguing that it could not be studied empirically but only through subjective means: 'We know of no scientifically ascertainable ideas. To be sure, that makes our efforts more arduous than in the past, since we are expected to create our ideas from within our breasts in the very age of subjective culture.'

LEFT: **Weber believed there were four distinct constituents of sociology, which he defined as being a comprehensive science of social action.**

'Social stratification'

Of all the essays and books Weber produced, *The Protestant Ethic and The Spirit of Capitalism* is the most celebrated. Here, he investigated the effect of religious ideas on economic activity and the relationship between them and what he termed 'social stratification'. He followed this up with books on the religions of China, India and on ancient Judaism. His studies of bureaucracy and authority were equally influential.

BIOGRAPHY

Name Max Weber

Born 1864

Place Erfurt

Nationality German

Key facts Lawyer, politician, historian, sociologist and economist, Weber was profoundly influential on social theory. He dealt with the rationalization, bureaucratization and disaffection associated with the rise of capitalism.

Died 1920

KEY WORKS

• *The Protestant Ethic and The Spirit of Capitalism*

• *Economy and Society*

J.M.E. McTaggart
1866–1925

An idealist metaphysician who won renown as one of Britain's leading authorities on Hegel, Cambridge philosopher J.M.E. McTaggart argued that there was no such thing as time, and whatever we perceive is actually an illusion.

BIOGRAPHY

Name J.M.E. McTaggart

Born 1866

Place London

Nationality British

Key facts Remembered today as the originator of a paradox designed to prove the unreality of time, McTaggart's contributions to metaphysics made him one of the leading British thinkers of the early 20th century.

Died 1925

KEY WORKS

- *The Unreality of Time*
- *The Nature of Existence*

Pursuing idealism

McTaggart was the top scholar of his year at Cambridge and, soon after graduating, was elected to a fellowship at Trinity College, where he remained as a lecturer in philosophy for the rest of his academic career. A leading member of the British Idealist school of philosophy, he was deeply influenced by the work of Hegel, although he criticized some of Hegel's conclusions. Later, he struck out on his own in his thinking, concluding that the world consisted of nothing but souls, each soul related to one or more of the others by love.

Together with G.E. Moore and Bertrand Russell he made up the intellectual trinity that dominated Cambridge philosophy in the early 1900s. After his Hegelian beginnings he developed an extremely personal idealist philosophy. Unlike many of his fellow idealists, he was unsympathetic to religion: 'If one was a Christian one would have to worship Christ, and I don't like him much. If you take what he said in the first three gospels (for St John's has no historical value, I believe), it is a horribly one-sided and imperfect ideal.' Ultimately, reality is best understood as consisting entirely of individual minds and their contents, making up a community of finite spirits. Each of these 'souls' was immortal, a premise that led him to defend the concept of reincarnation.

The unreality of time

However, it was his speculations about the nature of time that won McTaggart an enduring reputation. There was what he termed an A-series and a B-series – the former was concerned with past, present and future and the second with positions running from earlier to later. The latter could not exist without the former, so it was the A-series that made time possible. There was, he said, also a C-series, but, since this involved no change but simply governed order, it was not temporal.

McTaggart's conclusions were nothing if not radical. Time, he said, obviously involved change. He cited Queen Anne's death as an example. This, he wrote, 'was once an event in the far future. It became every moment an event in the nearer future. At last, it was present. Then it became past and will always remain past, though every moment it becomes further and further past.'

What McTaggart deduced from this was that, despite the seeming logicality of the progression, it contained an inherent contradiction. It presupposed the existence of the A-series in order to make it valid. The result was, he claimed, an 'infinite regression' or a vicious circle. The consequences were obvious. It meant that 'nothing that exists can be temporal and nothing existent can possess the quality of being in time'. In fact, there is no time. It is 'unreal and the appearance of temporal order is mere appearance'. It follows that all experience must be illusory.

Bertrand Russell

1872–1970

Probably Britain's most celebrated modern philosopher, Bertrand Russell won fame through his attempts to reduce mathematics to logic. Together with his Cambridge friend and colleague G.E. Moore, he is generally regarded as one of the founders of analytical philosophy.

Philosopher of principle

Russell was extremely well connected. He was the grandson of Lord John Russell, the Whig patrician who piloted the 1832 Reform Bill into law and served as one of Queen Victoria's prime ministers. Educated at home and then at Cambridge, where he studied mathematics and philosophy, Russell absorbed all his family's libertarian views. During the First World War, he was deprived of his Cambridge fellowship and sent to prison for his pacifism. In his later years, he played a prominent part in the founding of the Campaign for Nuclear Disarmament and was a vehement critic of US involvement in the Vietnam War.

In philosophy, his defence of logicism (the belief that mathematics can be reduced to logic), his theory of logical atomism and his theory of definite descriptions, which he regarded as his most important contribution to philosophical thought, are chief among his achievements.

Logic and analytical philosophy

According to his own account, Russell fell in love with mathematics as a young boy. 'From that moment on until Whitehead and I finished *Principia Mathematica* when I was 38, mathematics was my chief interest and my sole source of happiness.' It was not surprising, therefore, that his first major philosophical effort was to try to prove that arithmetic – and probably mathematics in its entirety – could be derived from basic logical principles. This was what *Principia Mathematica* was all about. It established Russell, second only to Gottlob Frege, as one of the great logicians of the century.

After this, Russell switched his efforts to different aspects of philosophy, applying the revolutionary new logical method he had devised to other philosophical problems, notably the question of knowledge. His starting point was the analysis of the language of seemingly run-of-the-mill statements. It involved close examination of the propositions such statements contained, the terms and concepts they employed and all of their logical implications. The procedures he adopted were soon taken up by others.

The development marked the birth of a whole new way of thinking, becoming known as 'analytical philosophy'. It was tricky stuff, but the theory of definite descriptions Russell devised has stood the test of time. He proposed it in order to solve a celebrated philosophical conundrum: whether a sentence can be called true or false when it fails to refer. His ingenious solution was to postulate that such sentences consist of a conjunction of individual claims. By dividing up the sentence in question into its various propositions, it is possible to establish which are true and which are false. If one is false, the sentence must be false, regardless of whether the other propositions it contains are true.

Sense data

Another problem Russell faced was the question of how we know the nature of objects in the real world. What we apparently perceive, he argued, is deceptive, since appearances are continually shifting and changing. Russell termed these appearances 'sense data'. He tried to devise a new conception of what objects were, postulating that they were logical constructions built out of or inferred from sense-data.

BELOW: **By using mathematical logic to analyse statements in ordinary language, Russell inaugurated a revolution in thinking that was to lead directly to what became known as analytical philosophy.**

G.E. Moore
1873–1958

A contemporary of Bertrand Russell and Ludwig Wittgenstein, G.E. Moore preached what he called a 'common-sense philosophy', rejecting idealism and the empirical approach in favour of down-to-earth realism. With Russell, he was the co-founder of analytical philosophy.

Rejecting idealism

G.E. Moore – he hated his Christian names and never allowed them to be used – studied classics and what was then called moral science at Cambridge. Like Bertrand Russell and J.M.E. McTaggart, he became a prize fellow of Trinity College, where he began work on formulating his philosophy. After leaving Cambridge in 1904 he worked independently on various philosophical projects, returning to the university seven years later and remaining there for the rest of his career. After retirement, he taught at universities in the USA as a visiting professor.

He rejected the tenets of absolute idealism and empiricism in favour of a more realistic approach, using ordinary language and rooted in common sense. In ordinary language, said Moore, questions of meaning and truth scarcely ever arise, since we know how to understand and use what we say. Indeed, he argued, there are many things that we know perfectly well, even though we lack the ability to say how we know them.

Moore advocated what he termed 'analysis of meanings' when it was necessary to probe deeper into the nature of concepts, definitions and the connections between them. The theory he put forward about them came to be known as the Identity Theory of Truth. Concepts, he said, could be analysed in one of two ways: split up into their constituent parts or, alternatively, defined in terms of their relationship with and distinction from other concepts.

Externals and ethics

With common sense as his yardstick, Moore attempted to deal with all sorts of philosophical problems, such as the question of whether 'external objects' – things not dependent on experience for existence – really existed. He argued that he could prove his point by simply showing that he had two hands. 'By holding up my two hands and saying as I make a certain gesture with the right hand "Here is one hand", and adding, as I make a certain gesture with the left "and here is another",' he believed that he had supplied what he said was 'rigorous proof' that an external world did exist. Moore's logical was impeccable, yet the proof was flawed, since, to postulate it, Moore had to presuppose that the external world existed. Nor did he show how he knew that his hands were mind-independent objects.

Moore also tried to explain what is good – the question, he said, lay right at the heart of ethics. This must always be an open question. To suppose otherwise would be to fall into 'the naturalistic fallacy', that is, confusing what is natural with what is considered to be good. In his view, good is a straightforward abstract property of which we are all aware. Goodness, however, is indefinable.

ABOVE: **Moore used the commonsense principles underpinning his philosophy to attack sceptics who argued that it was impossible to know anything about the world outside the mind.**

Ludwig Wittgenstein
1889–1951

One of the most important thinkers of the 20th century, Wittgenstein held that all philosophical problems stemmed from the misunderstanding of the logic of language. He believed that philosophy's sole aim was to bring about 'the greater clarification of thought'.

From Vienna to Cambridge

Born into a wealthy Jewish family, Wittgenstein started off studying as an engineer before his interest in the fundamentals of mathematics led him to take up philosophy. He became a pupil of Bertrand Russell at Cambridge and, after leaving the university in 1913, began the *Tractatus Logico-Philosophicus*, which, although only 70 pages long, took him years to complete. He worked on it while serving in the Austrian army during the First World War, and it was finally published in 1921. With it, he believed that he had solved all the problems philosophy had to offer and gave up the subject for some years. He returned to it, and Cambridge, in 1929, remaining there until he died of cancer in 1951.

Picture theory and logical form

His early speculations, which he embodied in the *Tractatus Logico-Philosophicus* – or *Tractatus*, as it is known (for such a short book, the full title is somewhat cumbersome; Wittgenstein adopted it at the suggestion of G.E. Moore) – concerned the relationship he felt existed between language, reality and thought. Wittgenstein claimed that it was language that lay at the heart of all thinking. It possessed an underlying logical structure that mirrored the logical structure of the world. He embodied this proposition in what became known as his 'picture theory' of meaning, in which he held that sentences were literally pictures or mirror images of actual or possible facts. It was language that allowed things to be expressed, sometimes clearly and sometimes not at all. 'What can be said at all can be said clearly,' he wrote, 'and what we cannot talk about we must pass over in silence.' Wittgenstein believed language marked the limit of thought. It was the logical relationship within it – what he termed 'logical form' – that enables us to represent reality accurately and talk meaningfully about the world.

Rethinking his philosophy

After giving up philosophy for a time, Wittgenstein began having doubts about whether he had really said the last word on the subject. In particular, he began to wonder if his picture theory was adequate. Language, it now seemed to him, could do many more things in addition to providing a picture of reality. Accordingly, Wittgenstein abandoned his picture metaphor and instead argued that language gained its meaning from the way in which it was employed. To this he linked his notion of what he termed a 'language game'. The concept is a complicated one to understand, but, broadly speaking, words, according to Wittgenstein's views, could be understood only in the context of the activities in which they were used. 'The meaning of a word,' he wrote, 'is its use in language.'

The *Tractatus* was the only work that Wittgenstein published in his lifetime; *Philosophical Investigations*, the book in which he substantially revised his thinking, appeared only after his death. By that time, he had long established himself as the driving force behind a whole new and revolutionary way of philosophical thinking. Not for nothing did Russell consider him the greatest intellect of his time.

ABOVE:
Wittgenstein claimed that philosophy's major problem was its failure to recognize the radically different ways in which language can be used.

Martin Heidegger
1889–1976

*One of the most controversial 20th-century philosophers because of his
ambivalent attitude to the Nazi dictatorship, Martin Heidegger was
an existentialist, whose main preoccupation was ontology – that is,
the study of being.*

BIOGRAPHY

Name Martin
Heidegger

Born 1889

Place Messkirch

Nationality German

Key facts Although
tainted by Nazi
associations, Heidegger
remains an influential
figure. His philosophy
changed over time,
becoming increasingly
obscure. It is not
surprising that he
remarked 'making
itself intelligible is
suicide for philosophy'.

Died 1976

KEY WORKS

• *Being and Time*

Politically controversial

Thwarted in his ambition to become a Jesuit priest through ill health,
Heidegger studied under Edmund Husserl at the University of Freiburg,
eventually being appointed rector there 1933, shortly after the Nazis took
power. His sympathy with National Socialism led to him being banned
from teaching after the Second World War. The ban was finally lifted in
1951, after which he continued formulating his thinking until his death.

Luckily for Heidegger, his philosophical speculations remained free
of the taint of Nazism. How far he was actually involved with National
Socialism is still a matter of debate, but he certainly joined the Nazi
Party, publically praised Hitler and repudiated Husserl, his old teacher,
as a Jew. Although he later fell out of favour with the regime, it was
enough to do lasting damage to his career, particularly when, after the
Second World War, he sought to excuse National Socialism by claiming
it to have been a massive social experiment, albeit one that had gone
horribly wrong.

The question of being

Like Wittgenstein, Heidegger's thinking changed over time – he himself
dated the change from the 1930s, labelling it *die Kehre* (the turn). His
later philosophy was much less systematic and frequently more obscure
than his earlier speculations.

In his earlier thinking, Heidegger's fundamental concern was with
what he termed 'the question of being'. He maintained that modern man
had become alienated from his primitive being; his aim, he stated, was to
uncover and rethink being in its proper light. Heidegger started by giving
'being' a name: *Dasein*. Literally translated, this means simply 'being there',
but, in Heidegger's context, it is better rendered as 'the entity which each
of us is' or 'being in the world'. It was, he stated, a 'new view of the basic
constitution of the human being', even though it had its roots deep in

> 6 *Thinking begins only when we have come to know that reason, glorified for centuries, is the stiff-necked adversary of thought.* 9

the past in the speculations of the pre-Socratic philosophers of ancient Greece. Heidegger argued that *Dasein* was the necessary foundation on which everything else depended.

Being and time

It was clear to Heidegger that the existence of which we have immediate awareness is naturally our own. From this, he argued that the best way forward was to analyse what it is we are aware of when we are aware of our own existence. 'We ourselves are the entities to be analysed,' he wrote.

This is where *Being and Time*, his philosophical masterpiece, starts. It reached a startling conclusion, with Heidegger arguing that, in all critical aspects, the human mode of being consisted of a threefold structure that corresponded to past, present and future time. In the final analysis, therefore, Heidegger postulated that being is time, and time is being. The two were interchangeable.

Understanding *Dasein*

Heidegger's speculations about the nature and purpose of *Dasein* were equally fascinating. He insisted, for instance, that it was aware of its own fate and the fact that it was mortal. This, he said, accounted for human *Angst* (dread). There was, however, another side to the coin. *Dasein* will always choose to make something out of nothing; it is alive to future possibilities, even if one of these is inescapable. This, of course, is death.

ABOVE:
Heidegger's intellectual reputation suffered after the Second World War because of the apparent support he had given the Nazis in the 1930s.

Rudolf Carnap
1891–1970

One of the leading members of the Vienna School and an influential force in logical positivism, Carnap fled Europe to escape Nazi persecution for his Jewish faith. He ended up in the USA, where he became an American citizen and remained until his death.

Relying on language

Carnap studied philosophy, mathematics and physics at the universities of Jena and Freiburg before moving to Vienna after the First World War. He fled Europe for the USA in 1935, where he became a dominant figure in post-war American philosophy.

Carnap's rise to philosophical prominence began after he was invited to join the Vienna School of thinkers, which, initially, had come together to study the work of Wittgenstein. In 1928 he published *The Logical Structure of the World*, his first major book, in which he argued that scientific terms were definable through phenomenologistic language. Over 20 other studies were to follow.

Also in 1928 came *Pseudoproblems in Philosophy*, in which Carnap argued that many philosophical problems were simply meaningless; they were the result, he said, of the misuse of language. Both books won him considerable philosophical renown for the rigour with which he expressed his views and the logic he employed to develop them.

Verification, meaning and logic

'Philosophy', Carnap wrote, 'is to be replaced by the logic of science – that is to say, by the logical analysis of the concepts and sentences of the sciences, for the logic of science is nothing more than the logical syntax of the language of science.' This language could be no ordinary language, since that in itself was ambiguous and so open to misunderstanding. Instead, he advocated the use of artificial languages, governed by the rules of logic and mathematics.

Like the other logical positivists, Carnap was guided in his thinking by the so-called 'verifiability principle'. This states that a synthetic statement is meaningful only if it can be verified. As he worked on, however, Carnap realized that the principle was insufficient for his purposes as it stood. What was needed was a new basic language – he

called it 'object language' – in which all primitive terms were physical and all other ones defined by use of primitive terms.

What emerged was a new verifiability principle. It stated that 'all terms must be reducible, by means of definitions or reduction sentences, to observational language'. This, too, was later shown to be inadequate, so Carnap started to develop yet another proposition. A term, Carnap now said, was meaningful only in the context of a given theory and language. Contrary to his previous thinking, he also admitted that some theoretical terms could be reduced to observational language and that there was a connection, albeit a tenuous one, between the two of them.

Such speculations had a major impact on the subsequent course of philosophical development, even if some of them have not stood the test of time completely. So, too, did Carnap's postulations on logic. He championed the use of inductive logic, that is, a logic that examines the logical relationships between statements and evidence. Its use would mean that, although still no one could be sure whether a hypothesis was true, what he called its 'degree of confirmation' could be rated and assessed.

ABOVE: **Carnap was a leading logical positivist, who believed that anything apparently contributing to human knowledge had to be verified for validity before it could be accepted.**

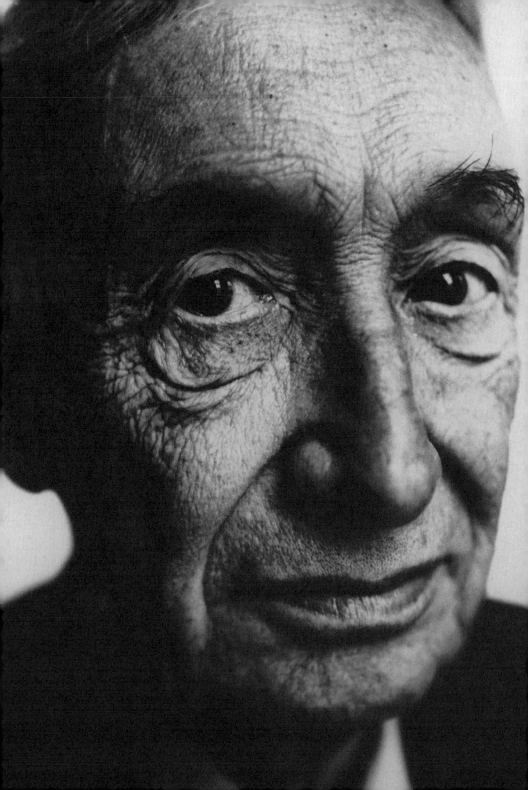

The Post-Modern Era

Mid 1950s–present day Although the term post-modernism was not coined until 1978, when the French thinker Jean-François Lyotard first used it, its roots lie further back than that.

Some have claimed that Nietzsche and Heidegger were, in some respects, precursors of post-modernism. Others say, in France at any rate, it originated with the structuralist revolution of the mid 1950s and early 1960s, when some philosophers began to argue that any statement of any kind was simply nothing more than an exercise in language.

From the 1950s onwards, philosophy has gone through a seismic change. To a large extent, this was a consequence of the scientific revolution that followed Albert Einstein's formulation of his theory of relativity. All scientific knowledge, it appeared, now had to be considered conjectural. The only certain thing was uncertainty. Karl Popper, in many people's eyes the leading philosopher of the day, argued that the same applied to political and social thought.

Max Horkheimer

1895–1973

The leader of the Frankfurt School – a group of philosophers and social thinkers who worked at the Institute of Social Research in Frankfurt am Main – Horkheimer is best known for his pioneering development of what he termed 'critical theory'.

Turning philosophy into a science

In defiance of his businessman father, Horkheimer studied at the University of Frankfurt, where he eventually became Professor of Social Philosophy and head of the Institute of Social Research. With the rise o the Nazis he was driven into exile, taking refuge in America, where he remained until 1949, after which he returned to Frankfurt, remaining there until his retirement.

His main interest was in social philosophy. His aim in his thinking was clear: 'to pursue the great philosophical questions using the most finely honed scientific methods, reformulate the questions, state things precisely, think of new methods and yet never lose sight of the general'.

The alleviation of suffering

In Horkheimer's view, social philosophers should focus first and foremost on two aspects of their subject: their philosophy had to be practical (its aim should be to 'alleviate suffering'); it should also work towards a 'reformation of the old question concerning the connection of particular existence and universal reason'.

RIGHT: **Horkheimer believed**

Herbert Marcuse

1898–1979

The 'father of the New Left', Marcuse won worldwide renown – and notoriety – as a radical philosopher, social theorist and political activist. Although he criticized Communism as well as capitalism, his main call was for the overthrow of the repressive affluent society.

Father of the left

A pupil of Martin Heidegger, Marcuse began his rise to prominence as a member of the Frankfurt-based Institute of Social Research. He fled to the USA in 1934 to escape Nazi persecution as a Jew and remained there for the rest of his life, teaching at several US universities.

Marcuse found his own radical voice in the mid 1950s with the publication of *Eros and Civilization*. In it, he attempted to synthesize Marx and Freud, while at the same time setting out his vision of a liberated non-repressive Utopian society, which, he said, would be free of the shackles of the past. *One-Dimensional Man* is generally accepted as his masterpiece, even though it was criticized by orthodox Marxists because it attacked Communism as well as capitalism.

An Essay on Liberation, celebrating liberation movements from the hippies to the Viet Cong, followed. With its publication, Marcuse's place as leader of the American intellectual left was secured. Although his influence is less now than it was, he is still regarded as one of the most influential radical theorists of his time.

LEFT: **A leading member of the Frankfurt School, Marcuse developed a model for critical social theory.**

BIOGRAPHY

Name Herbert Marcuse

Born 1898

Place Berlin

Nationality German, later American

Key facts A philosopher who celebrated the liberation and counterculture movements of the day, Marcuse was a trenchant critic of 'advanced industrial society', arguing that it was 'one-dimensional', oppressive and should be overthrown.

Died 1979

KEY WORKS

- *Eros and Civilization*
- *One-Dimensional Man*
- *An Essay on Liberation*

Gilbert Ryle

1900–1976

An influential Oxford-based thinker who followed Wittgenstein in advocating linguistic analysis as the way forward for philosophical thought, Ryle had a major impact on the development of what is known as 'ordinary language' philosophy.

BIOGRAPHY

Name Gilbert Ryle

Born 1900

Place Brighton

Nationality British

Key facts Ryle approached philosophy somewhat like map-making, arguing that philosophical problems could be solved, even eliminated, by examining and analysing the subtleties of ordinary language and making certain it was employed correctly.

Died 1976

KEY WORKS

- *The Concept of Mind*
- *Dilemmas*

An analyst of language

Educated at Oxford, Ryle became a lecturer there and eventually Waynflete Professor of Metaphysical Philosophy, a position he held for 25 years.

Ryle's conviction that linguistic analysis was the key to solving all major philosophical problems was one he consistently applied as he developed his own thinking. From early on in his career he argued that philosophical analysis of ordinary language could clarify thought. Philosophy's function, he believed, was to map the logical geography that he felt was an inherent factor in all conceptual thinking.

Category mistakes

What it was necessary to avoid – in everyday language as much as in philosophical speculation – was what he called 'category mistakes'. Suppose, for example, you are a factory manager taking some visitors around your plant. You show them the machine shops, the boiler rooms and the storage facilities. At the end of the tour, however, the visitors say: 'Yes, this is all impressive, but when are we going to see the plant?' They, Ryle would say, have committed a category mistake. The unspoken supposition is that the plant is something further to what you have shown them, whereas what you have, in fact, shown them actually makes up the plant. Put another way, the visitors are making the error of thinking the plant has the property of being one of the elements within itself.

> *A myth, of course, is not a fairy story. It is the presentation of facts belonging to one category in the idioms appropriate to another.*

Ryle believed that category mistakes were a major source of philosophical confusion. He accused Descartes of making just such an error when he put forward the notion that human beings possess tangible bodies and intangible minds. This, he said, was nonsense. Descartes had fallen into the trap of describing the mind, which is in one category, in language that was only appropriate for another category, the body. According to him, Cartesian Dualism was – in his celebrated phrase 'the ghost in the machine' – a myth.

Ryle and behaviourism

It was perfectly adequate, Ryle said, for descriptions of human behaviour never to refer to anything but the operation of the human body. This way of thinking became known as 'logical behaviourism'.

Ryle made considerable efforts to prove his point. In *The Concept of Mind* he noted that, although traditional language divided the inner, or mental, aspects of human life from the outer, or bodily, ones, any attempt to describe the inner aspect invariably fell back on the language of bodily motion and interaction. The only way forward, Ryle concluded, was to draw analogies from physical processes. Any statements about perception, emotion, belief, memory and so forth were no more than convenient shorthand ways of describing identifiable behaviour. To say that someone is angry, for instance, is not to describe their inner mental state but to describe their disposition to behave in a certain way.

At the time Ryle's theories impacted heavily on two separate, although related, schools of thought, the out-and-out logical behaviourists, such as Rudolf Carnap, and the 'ordinary language' philosophers, the most notable of whom was John Langshaw Austin. Today, however, most philosophers reject behaviourism because of the convincing examples that have been raised to refute it.

ABOVE: **For Ryle, it was philosophy's task to resolve the apparent problems caused by misunderstanding the concepts used to formulate them. He called these errors 'category mistakes'.**

Hans-Georg Gadamer

1900–2002

The driving force of modern hermeneutics – the philosophy of understanding and interpretation – Gadamer, although relatively little known outside Europe, rose to become one of the major philosophical figures of his time.

Science, meaning and experience

Gadamer was a pupil of Martin Heidegger; he said that he owed everything to the influence of his master. He himself was a distinguished academic, eventually succeeding Karl Jaspers as Professor of Philosophy at the University of Heidelberg, where he taught for more than 50 years.

Gadamer attacked the notion – held particularly by the logical positivists – that scientific method was the means that should be employed to establish truth. On the contrary, science, since it was performed by humans, could not be anything but subjective. The truths of history, culture and society could be discovered only through a kind of dialogue – listening to history as it was revealed in traditions and institutions, and culture as it was expressed in art, particularly poetry. Science had no part to play in such a revelation.

When it came to meaning, Gadamer saw it as dependent on experience, with language as its source. All human beings, he argued, were, by definition, an integral part of language, which grew and changed with them. He also held that conversation, or dialogue, was the basic model of understanding.

RIGHT: **Gadamer believed that the chief task of philosophy was 'to defend practical and political reason against the domination of technology-based science'.**

Jacques Lacan
1901–1981

Arguably the most important psychoanalyst since Freud, Lacan's groundbreaking development of psychoanalytical theory impacted on many other intellectual disciplines, including linguistics, structuralism, phenomenology and feminism.

BIOGRAPHY

Name Jacques Lacan

Born 1901

Place Paris

Nationality French

Key facts Lacan's first major paper, *On the Mirror Stage and the Formation of the I*, was published in 1936. From this, his reputation for unorthodoxy grew until, in 1962, he was barred from the International Psychoanalytical Association.

Died 1981

KEY WORKS

• *Écrits*

Psychological innovation

Lacan's developing thinking owed much to two modern philosophers, Karl Jaspers and Martin Heidegger, and the historical examples of Spinoza and Hegel. He also argued passionately for the need for 'a return to Freud'. Psychoanalysis, he believed, should question whether human actions were ever logically and rationally driven. Like Freud, he managed to transform the way we think about ourselves and how we assess our place within society.

Thanks to Lacan's efforts, psychoanalysis was reinstated at the cutting edge of critical theory. His belief that the unconscious was structured like a language, his theory of what he termed the 'mirror phase' and its role in the formation of the ego, and his complex notion of how a subject comes to identify himself or herself as 'I' in the social world all proved to be immensely influential. Lacan also devised what he termed 'ethics for our time', which, he hoped, would prove capable of dealing with the 'discontent of civilization', while his development of Freud's theory of sexual difference opened up new fields of debate in women's and gender studies.

RIGHT: **Whilst some believed Lacan to be the most significant psychoanalyst since Freud, others dismissed him as a charlatan.**

149

Karl Popper

1902–1994

Generally considered to be one of the greatest philosophers of science of the 20th century, Popper was also an influential social and political thinker. He staunchly defended what he termed the 'open society' and was an implacable opponent of totalitarianism in all its forms.

Upholding freedom

The son of a prosperous Viennese lawyer, Popper studied at the city's university, becoming a secondary-school teacher before deciding to devote himself to philosophy full time. The Nazi threat forced him to leave Austria, first for New Zealand, where he taught philosophy until the end of the Second World War, and then Britain, where he joined the London School of Economics, remaining there for the rest of his career. As a young man he had flirted with Communism, but he soon became disenchanted. His dislike of it was a central theme of *The Open Society and Its Enemies*, the second volume of which is devoted to a devastating criticism of Marx and Marxism.

Science and knowledge

The young Popper lived at a time of scientific turmoil, when, thanks to the theories of Albert Einstein, all the old certainties of Newtonian science were under threat. Popper was quick to challenge the conventional empirical consensus that scientific theories could be proven to be true, arguing that, even when a scientific principle had been repeatedly and successfully tested, it did not necessarily follow that it was correct; rather, it simply meant that it had not been proved false. Popper labelled this supposition the 'theory of falsification'. What was needed, he said, was a clear dividing line between what he defined as 'good science', that is, one in which theories are constantly challenged, and what he contemptuously called 'pseudoscience', one in which such a procedure was impossible to execute. All truly scientific hypotheses, he argued, had to be ready to stand trial in 'the court of experience'.

Popper went on to present a full-blown theory of knowledge. He argued that reality exists independently of the human mind. It also radically differs from human experience. For these reasons it can never be fully or directly understood. The only way to proceed is to take a pragmatic view as to what

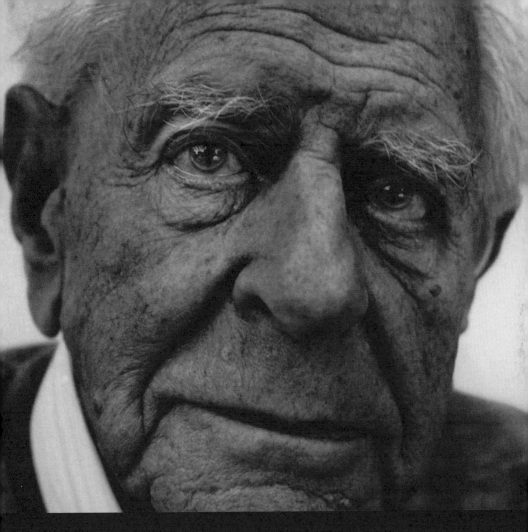

can and what cannot be accomplished. Instead of striving to find new certainties to add to existing ones, the best we can do is to replace existing theories with better ones, as there is no such thing as lasting certainty.

Popper and politics

Popper eventually realized that what applied to science was equally relevant to political and social theory. There was, he said, no such thing as certainty in politics and society. Any system of government that seeks to impose a single point of view on its citizens is unjustifiable, especially if criticism is disallowed and dissent actively repressed. What he defined as an 'open society' – one in which critical debate is allowed and opposition tolerated – is not only preferable but also more effective. It is the best way of managing the process of endless change, which Popper said, is what modern society is all about.

ABOVE: **Popper believed that, just like scientific knowledge, political and social theory were both permanently open to revision in the light of experience.**

Jean-Paul Sartre

1905–1980

Quite likely the best-known philosopher of the 20th century, Sartre dominated French intellectual life from immediately before the Second World War until his death nearly 50 years later. He is generally regarded as the father of modern existentialist thought.

BELOW: **Sartre believed that becoming aware of one's own freedom led to anxiety and acting in 'bad faith'.**

Intellectual polymath

Having studied in Paris and at various German universities, Sartre became a philosophy teacher before being called up to serve in the French army in 1939. Taken prisoner by the Germans in 1940, he was eventually repatriated. Later, he joined the French Resistance. After the

war he became a full-time writer and philosopher. A noted novelist, playwright and a controversial political figure because of his left-wing views, as well as a highly original thinker, he became one of the most respected figures in French cultural life.

Human destiny

Being and Nothingness is Sartre's most important philosophical work. In it, he described what he defined as the two types of being: *pour soi* (for itself) and *en soi* (in itself). He was indebted to Hegel for the terminology. He went on to define what he termed 'nothingness' or 'non-being' and to outline some of the key facets of existentialism. The central tenet of his thinking was that 'existence precedes essence', by which he meant that we actually create ourselves. What we eventually become is a construct, built and rebuilt out of experience and behaviour. We, and we alone, are responsible for ourselves and all the things we do.

This was a heavy burden, said Sartre. More often than not it can lead to feelings of anguish, abandonment and despair. In short, he said, 'we are condemned to be free'. As this was inevitable, the thing to do was to make the best of things. Human life demanded total commitment to a path, the significance of which always remained open to question and doubt.

Sartre said that 'the destiny of man is placed within himself', which meant the willing acceptance of such emotions as the price for achieving genuine human dignity. Above all, he warned, we must avoid what he termed *mauvaise foi* (bad faith), deluding ourselves into a state in which we can avoid the responsibility for what we do.

Politics and society

Sartre, however, did not concern himself solely with the individual self and its relationship to human freedom. In *Critique of Dialectical Reason*, his last major work which he left unfinished, Sartre revised his original existentialist posture. What he was trying to reconcile were two potentially conflicting viewpoints: his faith in Marxism and his existentialist beliefs. The result was a powerful synthesis of the two. He concluded that, after all, individual freedom was governed by historical, political and social circumstances. Indeed, it was what he called the group struggle that was the animating principle of human history.

What kind of society Sartre hoped would emerge was unclear. Despite his faith in Marxism, it certainly was not a Communist one. He was, he said, 'an anarchist' and a 'libertarian socialist'. The ideal society, so it would appear, would be based on two guiding principles: individual freedom and the elimination of material scarcity. How this was to be brought about, however, Sartre never said.

BIOGRAPHY

Name Jean-Paul Sartre

Born 1905

Place Paris

Nationality French

Key facts Sartre's influences included Descartes, Kant, Marx, Kierkegaard, Husserl and Heidegger. Nevertheless, his own highly original thought possessed a clarity and force all of its own, perfectly mirroring the prevailing spirit of his times.

Died 1980

KEY WORKS

- *Being and Nothingness*
- *Existentialism and Humanism*
- *Critique of Dialectical Reason*

Ayn Rand
1905–1982

Bestselling novelist, controversial polemicist and radical thinker, Russian-born Ayn Rand divided the philosophical world with her passionate advocacy of her self-devised philosophy of objectivism. She was dismissed by some as nothing more than a 'pop' philosopher.

BIOGRAPHY

Name Ayn Rand

Born 1905

Place St Petersburg

Nationality Russian, later American

Key facts Her aim was 'to provide men – or those who care to think – with an integrated, consistent, rational view of life'. Objectivity, the philosophical system she devised, was, she suggested, the complete answer.

Died 1982

KEY WORKS

• *The Virtue of Selfishness*

• *Introduction to Objective Epistemology*

• *The Romantic Manifesto*

Advocate of objectivism

Although she studied at the University of Petrograd (the name given to St Petersburg during the First World War), Rand was not an academic. Nor did she fit the conventional stereotypes of orthodox philosophy. Her thinking was straightforward and unconventional and resulted in the development of her philosophy of objectivism.

Disenchanted with post-revolutionary Russia, Rand left for the USA in 1925, where she got a job as a Hollywood screenwriter. Later, she became a successful novelist – *The Fountainhead* and *Atlas Shrugged* were both bestsellers. Her philosophical ideas, which she embodied in both novels, also attracted considerable public attention. They encompassed ethics, morals, politics, economics and theories of concepts and aesthetics.

Understanding objectivity

The basic premise on which Rand's philosophy was formulated was clear and simple: 'It begins with the axiom that existence exists, which means that an objective reality exists independent of any perceiver or of the perceiver's emotions, feelings, wishes, hopes or fears.' Objectivity, she claimed, 'holds that reason is man's only means of perceiving reality and his one guide to action. By reason, I mean the society which identifies and integrates the material provided by man's senses.'

These were far-reaching propositions. They were also attractive. They encouraged faith in rational self-interest and self-responsibility, resting on the core belief that no man is any other man's slave. Its advocacy of individualism, the need for constitutional protection of individual rights to life, liberty and property and its call for the powers of government to be strictly limited made it a logical continuation of the old-style liberal tradition of political philosophy. Objectivism, Rand said, was all-embracing and all-encompassing. It was a complete philosophy of life.

Ethics and morals

When it came to human ethics, Rand started from the viewpoint that any ethical system had to be 'based on and derived, implicitly or explicitly, from a metaphysic'. She then asserted that 'the ethic derived from objectivism holds that, since reason is man's basic tool of survival, rationality is his highest value. To use his mind to perceive reality and to act accordingly is man's moral imperative.'

What Rand did was to stand the traditional view of ethics, with its stress on the importance of unselfishness and concern for others, on its head. 'Objectivist ethics,' she wrote, 'in essence hold that man exists for his own sake, that the pursuit of his own happiness is his highest moral purpose, that he must not sacrifice himself to others, nor sacrifice others to himself.'

Politics and economics

Rand turned selfishness into a virtue. According to her reasoning, individual happiness was the highest end to which anyone could aspire, while self-sacrifice was immoral. Work and achievement, Rand said, were the highest goals in life. Politically, she called for the role of government to be reduced to an absolute minimum: 'The government should be concerned only with those issues which involve the use of force. Everything else should be privately run.' She applied the same reasoning to economics, arguing that only the free-market economic system could be considered moral.

BELOW: **Rand's philosophy proposed that the purpose of life was the pursuit of happiness.**

6 *Contradictions do not exist. Whenever you think you are facing a contradiction, check your premises. You will find one of them is wrong.* 9

Hannah Arendt

1906–1975

One of the most influential political theorists of her time, Arendt took as her theme some of the most significant political events of the day, using them to demonstrate the need to protect fundamental human rights at all costs.

A political philosopher

Arendt studied with Heidegger, with whom she had a passionate, but brief, affair before moving to Heidelberg to study under Karl Jaspers. Banned as a Jew from teaching in Germany by the Nazis, she moved to Paris and then, after the fall of France, to the USA. She taught at several notable universities – including Princeton, where she became the first ever female full fellow – and at the New School for Social Research in New York.

What makes Arendt's contributions to the subject problematic to assess is the fact that she never formulated a systematic expression of her views. Her writings cover many major and diverse topics such as totalitarianism, revolution, the nature of freedom, the human faculties of thinking and judging and the history of political thought. At bottom, what concerned her most was questioning the nature of politics and political life as distinct from all other areas of human activity.

Totalitarianism and terror

Naturally enough, Arendt was deeply influenced by the political events of her times. As a young political activist she had been forced to flee Germany in the face of Nazi persecution, so she had first-hand experience of totalitarianism in its most virulent form. Drawing on the Nazi example and that of Stalin's brutal reign of terror in Soviet Russia, she said that both regimes epitomized political evil.

Under Hitler and Stalin, terror, Arendt stated, ceased to be an instrument of state policy; it became an end in itself. What was to terrify her was what she termed the 'banality' of such evil. Writing about the trial of Adolf Eichmann for his part in implementing the 'final solution to the Jewish problem', she concluded that he was seemingly incapable of the self-judgement that would have made him aware of the nature of his deeds. He did not think or question. He simply obeyed.

Pursuing freedom

Arendt went on to examine the reason why totalitarianism had such a broad appeal. It was, she argued, because it offered a single clear and unambiguous idea to a disenchanted and disaffected people that accounted for their present woes and promised them a future free from danger and insecurity. In both Germany and Russia, she added, existing society had sown the seeds of its undoing, notably by allowing the 'usurpation of the state' by the bourgeoisie in pursuit of its own narrow interests at the expense of democracy, freedom and liberty.

Arendt argued that finding a satisfactory solution to this meant going back to the origins of democracy in ancient Greece and discovering how, slowly but surely, modern society had atrophied its values. She postulated that by reasserting them, by leading what she termed the *vita activa* (active life), it would once again be possible for freedom to be 'a character of human existence in the world'.

ABOVE: **As a Jew who had been forced to flee Germany to escape Nazi persecution, Arendt devoted her life to attacking all types of totalitarianism.**

Maurice Merleau-Ponty

1908–1961

A friend and close associate of Jean-Paul Sartre until they quarrelled over Sartre's unquestioning support of Communism, Maurice Merleau-Ponty argued it was only human perception that enabled us to develop an understanding of and engagement with the world.

Relying on perception

One of the foremost French philosophers of the period during and after the Second World War, Merleau-Ponty became the youngest ever professor of philosophy at the Collège de France in Paris in 1952.

He was a committed phenomenologist. Drawing on the example of Husserl and the existentialist outlook of Heidegger and Gabriel Marcel, he set out to demonstrate that empiricism and rationalism, the two traditional approaches to philosophy, were both fundamentally flawed and therefore valueless. Only phenomenological perception, Merleau-

6 *Truth does not inhabit only the inner man, or more accurately, there is no inner man, man is in the world, and only in the world does he know himself.* 9

Ponty argued, could provide a way of probing and analysing the nature of human existence. 'All consciousness is perceptual,' he wrote. 'The perceived world is the always-presumed foundation of all rationality, all value and all existence.'

Meno's paradox

To prove his point, Merleau-Ponty said that neither of the established philosophical disciplines could solve Meno's paradox, an invention of Plato's, who put it forward in one of his dialogues. Meno asks Plato: 'How can you look for something when you don't know what it is? Even if you come right up against it, how will you know that what you have found is the thing you didn't know?' Neither school, said Merleau-Ponty, could devise a satisfactory answer. 'Empiricism,' he wrote, 'cannot see that we need to know what we are looking for, otherwise we would not be looking for it.' As for what he termed 'intellectualism' – his preferred term for rationalism – it 'fails to see that we need to be ignorant of what we are looking for, or, equally again, we should not be searching for it'.

Empiricists, Merleau-Ponty concluded, were guilty of 'experience error', that is, of accepting what prior concepts decreed should be the answer. Rationalism was just as problematic. It assumed that all knowledge is known a priori – that is, prior to experience. If, however, we already know what we are trying to discover, why bother searching for it?

Phenomenological perception

Merleau-Ponty devoted all his philosophical efforts to asserting perception's primacy over the other philosophical systems he so condemned. He started with the bold assertion that experience consisted of a dialogue between subject and object, and any meaning derived from it comes about by virtue of what he termed our 'embodied state'. It allows us to perceive things as cold and hot, near and far, big and little and so on. Similarly, the way in which we experience time is governed by the body's inability to be anywhere else other than the present.

Merleau-Ponty's parallel assertion was just as bold. For him, the body was not simply a machine manipulated by the brain, nor was consciousness simply something that went on in the head. Rather, he said, it is experienced in and through the 'lived body'. It is 'made of the same flesh as the world, and it is because the body is the flesh of the world that we can know and understand the world'. It was the necessary 'third link' between subject and object. The circle was squared. The philosophy of perception was complete.

BIOGRAPHY

Name Maurice Merleau-Ponty

Born 1908

Place Rochefort-sur-Mer

Nationality French

Key facts Philosophically, Merleau-Ponty rejected the prevailing disciplines of empiricism and idealism, advocating instead a system of thought based firmly on phenomenology.

Died 1961

KEY WORKS

- *Phenomenology of Perception*

LEFT: **Merleau-Ponty argued that all human experience was based upon a subject-object dialogue and that there is an interdependence between the two.**

Simone de Beauvoir

1908–1986

The lifelong companion of Jean-Paul Sartre, whom she met while they were both students, de Beauvoir emerged as a great novelist and as a major philosopher in her own right. She was largely responsible for initiating the modern feminist movement.

From ethics to feminism

De Beauvoir passed her final examination at the Sorbonne at the age of 21 to become the youngest philosophy teacher in France. Her long relationship with Sartre influenced some of her thinking but she also made significant philosophical contributions of her own to the subject, first in the field of ethics and then as a feminist pioneer.

She started off by writing on ethics, taking the existentialist point of view and concerning herself particularly with the ethical responsibility the individual has for himself or herself, other individuals and the socially, politically and economically oppressed. Individual freedom, she said, required the freedom of others in order for it to be realized.

In 1948 de Beauvoir left ethics behind her. In that year she published *The Second Sex*, in which she investigated every major aspect of female oppression. Although some of the views she expressed were bitterly attacked by right- and left-wing critics – its subject matter was considered so controversial by the Vatican that it added the book to its notorious *Index of Prohibited Books* – the book was generally hailed as a masterpiece. It established de Beauvoir as the philosopher of feminism, a reputation she enjoyed for the rest of her life.

The 'eternal feminine'

In *The Second Sex* de Beauvoir started with the startling postulate that women have always been oppressed by men by their relegation to the status of what she termed 'the Other'. She held that a woman was 'the incidental, the inessential, as opposed to the essential. He is the Subject, he is the Absolute – she is the Other.' The whole relationship between the sexes was therefore fundamentally and perpetually unequal.

What de Beauvoir proposed to do was to investigate how this inequality had originated and what structures, attitudes and presuppositions helped

to maintain its social power. She was convinced of one inescapable fact: 'One is not born a woman but, rather, becomes one.' Woman does this by living the way a male-dominated society deems appropriate for her. She accepts, de Beauvoir said, the role of the 'eternal feminine'.

Liberating women

De Beauvoir put forward various demands, all of which, she said, had to be satisfied if women were to emancipate themselves. 'A modern woman prides herself on thinking, taking action, working, creating, on the same terms as men; instead of seeking to disparage them, she declares herself their equal.' Achieving this goal meant changing the existing social structure. She demanded the provision of universal childcare, equality in education, contraception, the legalization of abortion and, above all, what we today would term 'affirmative action' to ensure woman's economic freedom and independence from man.

This was the stuff of revolution, but, for some later feminists, it was misguided. They argued that, rather than liberating women, de Beauvoir was simply urging them to become more like men. However, nowhere did de Beauvoir say that male qualities are superior to female ones. What she did say is that only by achieving these ends can women become liberated

Willard Van Orman Quine

1908–2000

The dominant force in American philosophy from the 1950s, Quine won fame for his attack on the analytical/synthetic distinction between philosophical propositions that had been at the heart of philosophy since the time of Kant. He asserted that science was 'the final arbiter of truth'.

Logic, language and epistemology

Quine studied mathematics and logic at Oberlin College in his home state before winning a scholarship to Harvard. He spent his entire career teaching there, eventually becoming Edgar Pierce Professor of Philosophy from 1956 to 1978. He continued his connection with Harvard as an emeritus fellow right up to his death.

Although Quine began as a mathematical logician, it was as a philosopher of language and as an epistemologist that he made his lasting mark. He is widely held to have changed the way we think about language and its relation to reality, while he argued that epistemological theories should be 'naturalized'. By this he meant that, although such theories could still be used to deal with philosophical questions, their answers must take account of scientific facts. Above all, a-priori speculation had to be discarded and replaced by empirical explanation.

RIGHT: **Quine was a committed empiricist, who argued that it was impossible for any proposition to be independent of experience.**

Claude Lévi-Strauss
1908–2009

A pioneer of social anthropology, Lévi-Strauss was a structuralist who won fame through his groundbreaking investigation of myths, his reception of history and humanism and his refusal to accept that Western civilization was something unique.

Learning from primitive society

Although some might argue that Lévi-Strauss was not a philosopher at all, it is indisputable that his social anthropology had philosophical roots. Philosophy deeply influenced his study of myths. In it, he was indebted to the work of the Swiss philologist Ferdinand de Saussure, whose invention of the 'linguistic term' had a lasting impact on the course of 20th-century philosophical thinking.

Myths, men and society

Lévi-Strauss concluded that myths, although distinct in their individual content, shared a universal structure. He postulated that language encoded dualistic elements drawn from nature and culture, which are common to human experience. He also speculated that all people have the same intellectual potential, and that there was no such thing as a primitive or civilized mind.

RIGHT: **Celebrated as the pioneer of structuralist anthropology, Levi-Strauss applied what he learned from his researches into tribal myths to the study of the human mind.**

BIOGRAPHY

Name Claude Lévi-Strauss

Born 1908

Place Brussels

Nationality Belgian

Key facts It is as a social anthropologist rather than a philosopher that Lévi-Strauss made his name. His philosophy declares that all men are intellectually equal in their potential, and that there is a common denominator of human thought.

Died 2009

KEY WORKS

- *The Raw and the Cooked*
- *The Savage Mind*

Simone Weil

1909–1943

Philosopher, radical reformer and religious mystic, Simone Weil published just a few poems and articles during her lifetime. It was only after her death that she was recognized as one of the most original thinkers of her time. The poet T.S. Eliot called her "a woman of genius … akin to that of the saints."

RIGHT: **Throughout her turbulent career, Weil believed in the sanctity of labour. She held that work had to be suffused with meaning to be properly fulfilling.**

From Marxism to mysticism

Weil studied philosophy in Paris, where she quickly became known for her radical political views. After graduating, she alternated the teaching of philosophy with stints of manual labour. During the Second World War, she left France to escape the Nazis, going first to the USA and then to Britain, where she worked for the Free French until her death from tuberculosis and self-starvation at the age of only 34.

Simone Weil was an enigma. Born a Jew, she ended up fostering a mystical theology that came very close to Catholicism, although she never joined the church – she was, she said, a Platonic Christian. Her political position changed over time as well. As a student she was nicknamed the 'Red Virgin', but she later turned against Communism, denouncing the bureaucracy it had imposed on the state.

Where Weil was consistent was in her moral idealism and her almost fanatical devotion to her vision of social justice. Her identification with the working class was total. She gave most of what she earned as a teacher to the unemployed, and she spent months working in fields and factories in a Herculean effort to try to understand workers' real needs.

A.J. Ayer

1910–1989

Always 'Freddie' Ayer to his friends and associates, A.J. Ayer demonstrated his brilliance as a philosopher early in life. He published Language, Truth and Logic, *his greatest book, in 1936, when he was just 26 years old.*

Pursuing logical positivism

The rich son of wealthy parents, Ayer studied at Oxford before going to Vienna, where he absorbed the basics of logical positivism from the Vienna School. After a long period at the University of London following the Second World War, he returned to Oxford, where he became Wykeham Professor of Logic. A prolific broadcaster, magnetic lecturer and conversationalist and lifelong socialite, he knew everyone there was to know, from the Queen downwards.

His approach is evident in *Language, Truth and Logic*, in which his basic proposition was that a sentence could be meaningful only if it is verifiable through experience or self-evidently true or false. He considered metaphysical and religious statements belonged to neither group and so were meaningless.

Later in life Ayer modified and refined some of his ideas. Asked on television in 1979 what the main defects of his book were, he candidly replied: 'I suppose the most important defect was that nearly all of it was false.' Nevertheless, it is still regarded as a classic description of logical positivism and remains required reading for philosophy students all over the world today.

RIGHT: **Ayer was a logical positivist, who argued that all statements must be obviously true or false, or capable of empirical verification to be meaningful.**

BIOGRAPHY

Name A.J. Ayer

Born 1910

Place London

Nationality British

Key facts The leading British exponent of logical positivism, Ayer was a convinced empiricist who firmly believed that all statements about physical objects could be reduced to what he termed 'sense data'.

Died 1989

KEY WORKS

- *Language, Truth and Logic*
- *The Problem of Knowledge*
- *The Central Questions of Philosophy*

Alan Turing

1912–1954

A mathematical genius, wartime code breaker and pioneer of computer science, Alan Turing never classed himself as a philosopher. Nevertheless, the questions he raised in Computing Machinery and Intelligence *have continued to influence philosophy ever since he first posed them.*

BIOGRAPHY

Name Alan Turing

Born 1912

Place London

Nationality British

Key facts During the Second World War, Turing was one of those who cracked the German Enigma Code, later becoming a pioneer in the field of electronic computing.

Died 1954

Mathematical genius

Turing's early contributions to mathematical logic, made while he was a young Cambridge fellow, were immense. Famously one of the team that cracked the seemingly unbreakable Enigma Code used by the Germans during the Second World War, he also became one of the pioneers of computing and artificial intelligence after the war. Charged with committing a homosexual act in 1952, he killed himself two years later.

Although he probably would have laughed at the notion of being described as a philosopher, Turing's impact on the course of modern philosophy was immense. What he contributed to the subject was his new and rigorous theory of computationalism, which postulated that thought is a form of computation. Philosophers found that what Turing christened his 'imitation game', the Turing Test, was to tax their existing understanding of such fundamental philosophical concepts as consciousness, intelligence, mind, body, free will and predetermination.

KEY WORKS

• *Computing Machinery and Intelligence*

The 'imitation game'

Turing devised the game to find the answer to the question 'Can a machine think?' Philosophers would say that the question in itself was problematical, since it all depended on what was meant by the words 'machine' and 'think'. For this reason, Turing decided to get rid of the question and to devise a game to take its place.

The game has three players, each in a separate room, communicating with one another by means of teletype terminals. One of the players, the questioner, has to guess the sexes of the other two – one a man and the other a woman – through a question-and-answer dialogue. One attempts to confuse the questioner, while the other's task is to help him to guess his or her gender correctly.

Answering the question

Turing continued by asking what would happen if the second player – the one who is tasked with confusing the questioner – was replaced by a machine. Would the questioner guess more or less correctly than he would when the other players were people? Turing postulated that the answer would determine whether or not the machine could think – a machine sophisticated enough to remain undetected must possess the same intelligence as the person it is replacing. The conclusion is obvious: anything that responds intelligently must be classed as intelligent.

Turing believed the game's possible applications were limitless. To pass the test, he said, the machine had to possess knowledge and have the ability to use natural language, to reason and to learn. No machine has succeeded in meeting all these criteria – yet.

Turing's game has proved highly influential; it has also been widely criticized. Largely, this was because, critics said, it made the assumption that human beings can judge a machine's intelligence by comparing its behaviour with human behaviour. Turing himself, however, was quite clear as to the test's aim, which was not to fool the questioner but rather to show that an artificial intelligence could imitate the human one.

ABOVE: **Turing's pioneering work on artificial intelligence sparked off a continuing philosophical debate about the way in which the mind works and the nature of its processes.**

Donald Davidson

1917–2003

One of the most important American philosophers of the second half of the 20th century, Donald Davidson's brilliantly daring ideas broke new philosophical ground in fields ranging from semantic theory through to epistemology and ethics.

BIOGRAPHY

Name Donald Davidson

Born 1917

Place Springfield, Massachusetts

Nationality American

Key facts Davidson turned from classical to analytical philosophy, directing the bulk of his efforts to resolving one of the main philosophical issues of his time – how to understand who we are.

Died 2003

KEY WORKS

• *Essays on Actions and Events*

• *Inquiries into Truth and Interpretation*

• *Subjective, Intersubjective, Objective*

Revolutionising language

Educated at Harvard, where he studied under William Van Orman Quine, Davidson rose to fame as a leading philosopher relatively late in his career. He started by making important contributions to decision theory, one of his main propositions being that reasons explain actions inasmuch as they are the causes of those actions.

Davidson's prominence, however, really stems from his groundbreaking work on the philosophy of language, in which he attempted to ascertain, first, what meaning was and, second, to formulate a theory of meaning applicable to natural language. Formulating such a theory was a Herculean task. It meant developing a mechanism by which a philosopher could generate a theorem that specifies what each sentence means for every actual and potential sentence of the language in question. Davidson realized this involved generating an infinite number of theorems on the basis of a finite set of axioms. The meaning of sentences, he concluded, could be seen as depending on the meaning of their parts.

Belief in pragmatism

He went on to connect his theory of meaning with the theory of truth developed by the Polish philosopher Alfred Tarski. Although he adapted it substantially, it provided him with the formal framework on which his linguistic speculations and interpretations could be based.

As he progressed, Davidson's views became more and more radical. Ultimately, he came to believe that thought was not possible for beings lacking the linguistic means to express it. At heart, however, his approach was deeply pragmatic. Exploring the way in which language possesses meaning, he considered words in themselves had no meaning at all. Rather, he said, people engage in meaningful communication about the world in which they live and of which they are a part.

By agreeing with Ludwig Wittgenstein that social exchange was the basis of language, Davidson challenged the traditionalist position – formulated by Descartes with the maxim *cogito, ergo sum* (I think, therefore I am) – that an individual mind could by itself know about the world. Not only language but thought itself, he argued, was created by the interaction of the individual, all other people and the non-human universe.

A lasting influence

Such reasoning meant that there was no room for scepticism or relativism in Davidson's philosophy. They were, he said, simply incoherent. Nor were there any 'strict determinist laws on the basis of which mental events can be predicted or explained'. He concluded that 'laws are linguistic' and that 'events are mental only as described'.

What made Davidson particularly important in the philosophical context of his times was not simply his speculations themselves – exciting as these were – but the fact that they combined in such a way as to provide a single integrated approach to the problems posed by language, mind, action and knowledge. Although some have disputed the philosophical viability of his speculations, it seems likely that they will be of enduring significance.

ABOVE: **Davidson's impact on philosophy was immense. He held that there was 'no such thing as language, not if a language is anything like what many philosophers and linguists have supposed'.**

Peter Strawson

1919–2006

Oxford philosopher Peter Strawson was a leading champion of the so-called 'ordinary-language movement' in contemporary philosophy. His trenchant thinking was instrumental in re-establishing metaphysics at the centre of the philosophical stage.

Reviving metaphysics

BELOW: **Strawson said that he simply did not understand free will, that what he termed determinism was correct and that libertarians were guilty of 'panicky metaphysics'.**

Educated at Oxford, Strawson returned there in 1948 as a college tutor in philosophy after his war service and a brief stint teaching at the University College of North Wales. He was Waynflete Professor of Metaphysics from 1968 to 1987, the year of his retirement.

Strawson made his mark on the philosophical world with his reassertion of traditional values, most notably in metaphysics, where, although he disagreed with some of his propositions, he was largely responsible for rehabilitating the reputation of Immanuel Kant and

bringing Kantian idealism back into the mainstream of contemporary philosophy by suggesting new ways of interpreting his thinking.

Strawson was also a notable philosophical polemicist, making his name with his critique of Bertrand Russell's theory of descriptions, while, later, being equally critical of John Langshaw Austin's correspondence theory of truth. Some have seen the attack Strawson launched as part of the power struggle that was taking place in Oxford at that time between Austin, the leader of the so-called Oxford School, and Strawson, the young pretender. Strawson's criticisms were generally held to have wounded Austin's theory fatally.

Demolishing Russell

Strawson's criticism of Russell struck at the roots of a theory that had been considered a vital part of the logician's toolkit ever since it was first put forward in 1905. Strawson argued that the analysis Russell produced to support his speculations was demonstrably incorrect.

Take, for example, the sentence 'The King of France is bald'. According to Russell's analysis, what the sentence says is that at least one thing is king of France, at most one thing is king of France and that whatever is king of France is bald. The statement, therefore, is false. Strawson, however, argues that, on the contrary, since there is no such thing as the king of France, the sentence is neither true nor false. This was the result of what he refers to as a 'failure of reference'. He concluded Russell had failed to distinguish between a sentence and a statement and had confused mentioning with meaning.

An upholder of tradition

One of the factors influencing Strawson in his attack on Russell's long-held theory was his own conviction that it failed to do justice to the richness of ordinary language. This was something Strawson particularly cherished. He felt the same way about natural beliefs. In two seminal works – *Individuals*, which he published in 1959, and *The Bounds of Sense*, which followed in 1970 – he put forward a rational account of beliefs 'stubbornly held . . . at a primitive level of reflection'. Even if these were actually or apparently rejected by philosophers 'at a more sophisticated level of reflection', they were, he argued, what we all are 'naturally and inescapably committed to'.

Meticulous analysis of how human beings actually describe the world helped Strawson to achieve his goal of creating what he termed 'descriptive metaphysics'. It sparked off a transformation in thought that freed philosophy from the constrictions of positivism and linguistic analysis, and its impact has been enduring.

BIOGRAPHY

Name Peter Strawson

Born 1919

Place London

Nationality British

Key facts Few modern philosophers could be said to have changed the course of philosophical thinking, but Peter Strawson certainly did, famously attacking Bertrand Russell's theory of descriptions, saying that 'ordinary language has no exact logic'.

Died 2006

KEY WORKS

• *On Referring*

• *Individuals*

• *The Bounds of Sense*

• *Logico-Linguistic Papers*

• *Freedom and Resentment*

John Rawls

1921–2002

One of the most influential political philosophers since the Second World War, American thinker John Rawls propounded a theory of 'justice as fairness', in which he argued that the rights of individuals must take precedence over the common good.

BIOGRAPHY

Name John Rawls

Born 1921

Place Baltimore

Nationality American

Key facts In his work Rawls gave a new meaning to the concepts of justice and liberalism, putting forward an argument for a new social contract and a system of justice based on simple fairness for all.

Died 2002

KEY WORKS

- *A Theory of Justice*
- *Political Liberalism*
- *The Law of Peoples*

Avoiding the limelight

Educated at Princeton, Rawls taught there before moving to Cornell University, where he started developing what was to become his groundbreaking theory of justice. He took up a post at the Massachusetts Institute of Technology in 1960, two years later moving to Harvard, where he remained for the rest of his career.

John Rawls was a modest, intensely private man, who steadfastly resisted all attempts to drag him into the philosophical limelight. Attempts to praise him in person were uphill work, while offers of prizes, medals and honorary degrees were usually courteously, but firmly, declined. Nevertheless, his impact on political philosophy was profound and enduring. Rawls rescued philosophy from its preoccupation with dry-as-dust questions of logic, linguistics and the philosophy of science, focusing it again firmly on the fundamentals of ethics, social justice and the limits of freedom and responsibility.

'Justice as fairness'

From the outset of his career Rawls's thinking was guided by the need to find the answer to what is the most appropriate moral conception of justice for democratic society. His answer – which took him 30 years to expand, refine and perfect – was clear and simple: he called for the legal system to be reformed so that it would be fair for all and for the conclusion of a new social contract in which the rights of all minorities would be protected.

The proposal ran counter to the prevailing utilitarian viewpoint. Rather than agreeing that laws were just when they promoted the greatest good for the greatest number, Rawls argued completely opposite: 'Each person possesses an inviolability founded on justice that even the welfare of society as a whole cannot override.'

Guiding principles

Rawls formulated some basic principles to act as his starting point. The first, the Liberty Principle, stated that 'each person is to have an equal right to the most extensive scheme of equal basic liberties compatible with a similar scheme of liberty for others'. The second was the Justice Principle, which stated that every individual must be allowed to enjoy 'fair equality of opportunity'. Allied with this, Rawls put forward his Difference Principle, in which inequality was acceptable only if it benefited the worst off.

If there was a clash between the principles, the Liberty Principle, said Rawls, took preference. He was confident that together they were 'the principles that rational and free persons concerned to further their own interests would accept in a unified position of equality as defining the fundamentals of the terms of their association'. If necessary, he went on, they should be tested against common sense to bring them into what he called 'reflective equilibrium'.

Rawls's other great contribution to political philosophy was to restate and redefine the meaning of liberalism. In his *Political Liberalism*, he highlighted the differences between liberalism as a philosophy of life and its role as a political creed. The aim, he said, should be to achieve an 'overlapping consensus' between the two.

ABOVE: **Rawls rejected utilitarianism in favour of an updated social contract, in which the rights of the individual would be reconciled with the needs of the community, particularly the demands of justice.**

Thomas Kuhn

1922–1996

Probably the most influential scientific philosopher of the last century, Kuhn's groundbreaking theory of scientific revolution was a milestone in the evolution of modern scientific thought. It completely changed how we think about the nature of science and its development.

BIOGRAPHY

Name Thomas Kuhn

Born 1922

Place Cincinnati

Nationality American

Key facts According to Kuhn, rather than being a steady, cumulative acquisition of knowledge, science was 'a series of peaceful intervals punctuated by intellectually violent revolutions'.

Died 1996

KEY WORKS

• *The Structure of Scientific Revolutions*

Prophet of scientifc revolution

Kuhn began as a physicist but switched to studying the philosophy and history of science after completing his doctorate at Harvard. He later spoke of a 'eureka moment' that convinced him to make the change. He taught at Harvard, Berkeley and Princeton before becoming the Laurence Rockefeller Professor of Philosophy at the Massachusetts Institute of Technology. His theory of scientific revolution made him world famous.

Kuhn started developing a new philosophy of science early on his career, when asked to teach a course in the history of science to humanities students at Harvard. 'Until then,' he later recalled, 'I'd never read an old document in science.' What he discovered set him thinking. The immediate question he asked himself was why were Aristotle's ideas about matter and motion so very different from those of Newton? His answer was simple. Aristotle, he concluded, was not 'bad Newton', it was just different. This led him to react against the accepted view that science was a continuously progressive subject, always edging closer and closer towards the truth. Ultimately, he came up with a totally new theory to account for the course of scientific development.

> *It is, I think, particularly in periods of acknowledged crisis that scientists have turned to philosophical analysis as a device for unlocking the riddles of their field. Scientists have not generally needed or wanted to be philosophers.*

Paradigms and paradigm shifts

Periods of what Kuhn termed 'normal science'
revolved around the existence of a consensus
– what he called a paradigm – of prevailing
scientific perceptions. During such periods, most
scientists spend much of their time problem
solving. This situation, however, does not last for
ever. Revolutions, Kuhn said, occur, when, for
one reason or another, a paradigm shift takes
place, with the existing paradigm being
overthrown by a new one. It was impossible for
the new paradigm to be built on the preceding
one or co-exist with it; it could only supplant it,
since 'the normal-scientific tradition that emerges
from a scientific revolution is not only
incompatible but actually incommensurable
with that which has gone before'.

What Kuhn was arguing was that science
progresses in a cyclical pattern, alternating
periods of 'normal' and revolutionary
development. He turned to history to support his
point, citing as classic examples the Copernican
revolution, which overthrew the long-held
Ptolemaic notion that the sun revolved around
the earth, and Einstein's overturning of Newton's
theory of gravity, space and motion.

Incommensurability

Simultaneously, Kuhn put forward the notion of incommensurability to
account for his belief that there was no such thing as scientific progress
– at least not in the sense that previous thinkers had described it. His new
thesis challenged both positivist and realist concepts of scientific change.
The rejection of a previous paradigm in favour of a completely new one,
he said, inevitably rules out the possibility of a meaningful comparison of
the two. He again turned to history for support, arguing that scientists in
different historical periods operated in psychologically different worlds:
'Practising in different worlds the two groups of scientists see different
things when they look from the same point in the same direction.'

Although many philosophers criticized Kuhn violently at first, his
views soon proved highly influential. His notions spread from the
natural sciences to the social ones and then ultimately extended to
activities outside science altogether.

ABOVE: **Kuhn's
belief that science
moved on in fits and
starts, powered by
what he christened
paradigm-shifts, put
an end to the
long-established
notion of a
continuous progress
in the history of
scientific ideas.**

Paul Feyerabend

1924–1994

One of the most significant and controversial figures in modern scientific philosophy, Feyerabend argued that there were no rules governing scientific method. There was only one principle that mattered, he claimed, and that was 'anything goes'.

A philosophical maverick

BELOW: **Feyerabend believed that there were no valid rules to scientific method. If there were, he argued, scientific activity would be hindered and progress retarded.**

Badly wounded on the Eastern Front in 1944, Feyerabend studied singing and stage management before turning to philosophy, first in Vienna and then in London, where he was taught by Karl Popper. He became Popper's disciple, and studied under him for a time at the London School of Economics, although he later refuted Popper's views. He taught philosophy at the University of Bristol, then moved to California and Berkeley, where, although he passed through some tempestuous times, he was to remain, with spells at the Zurich Polytechnic, until his eventual retirement.

Feyerabend was a philosophical maverick – some of his many critics described him as more of a gadfly than a serious philosopher. 'Scientists,' he said, 'have more money, more authority, more sex appeal than they deserve. The most stupid procedures and the laughable results are surrounded by an aura of excellence. It is time to cut them down to size.' Science, Feyerabend insisted, simply was not rational and progressive as previous generations of philosophers had claimed. If there was progress, it was because some scientists were prepared to break all the rules in the book, adopting the principle that 'anything goes'. It was the one and only principle that Feyerabend believed could be defended under all circumstances in all the various stages of human development.

Feyerabend's conversion

Despite what his enemies later claimed, Feyerabend did not reach this conclusion lightly. It took him quite some time to renounce his initial empirical views. He started off as a logical positivist and an ardent admirer of his teacher Popper, even translating Popper's *The Open Society and its Enemies* into German. Later, however, he repudiated Popper for his advocacy of scientific rationalism – in particular the theory of falsification that Popper had postulated as a means of getting to the scientific truth. Feyerabend gradually came to believe that there was no such thing, holding that individual theories were simply not consistent with one another. Moreover, since there was no single scientific method, scientific success owed just as much to a mixture of subterfuge, rhetoric, conjecture, politics and propaganda as it did to rational argument.

Theoretical pluralism

What drove scientific research forward, Feyerabend argued, was the competition provided by a plurality of possible alternatives. He called this 'theoretical pluralism'. He then went even further, claiming that there were no such things as facts anyway, since, by definition, all factual statements were theory laden. What people consider to be facts, he maintained, ultimately depended on what they believed or wanted to believe. The best way forward was thus to select the theory that contributed the most to understanding.

He summed up his iconoclastic views in *Against Method*, which he published in 1975. Its appearance provoked a critical storm, but, even while he was being condemned by his peers, Feyerabend began to win a popular following. His belief that objectively there was little to choose between science and the claims of astrology, alternative medicine and even voodoo combined with his concern for green issues to make him a hero of the anti-technological counterculture of the time.

Michel Foucault

1926–1984

One of the most celebrated French philosophers of the latter half of the 20th century, Foucault's penetrating thoughts on language, mental illness, crime and sexuality widely influenced social scientists as well as helped to shape the course of French philosophy.

BIOGRAPHY

Name Michel Foucault

Born 1926

Place Poitiers

Nationality French

Key facts Drawing upon philosophy, history, psychology and sociology, Foucault attempted to demonstrate how power and knowledge interact to produce the human self.

Died 1984

KEY WORKS

- *Madness and Civilization*
- *Discipline and Punish*
- *The History of Sexuality*

Charting a new course

Foucault's father hoped that his son would become a doctor, but instead he studied philosophy and psychology. After spending some years abroad, he returned to France in 1960 to teach philosophy at the University of Clermont-Ferrand. In 1969, he became a professor at the Collège de France in Paris, a position he held until his death from an Aids-related illness in 1984.

Philosophically, Foucault was a structuralist who devoted much of his energy into mapping out a new course for French philosophy. He was also a noted political activist, campaigning tirelessly for the rights of the underdog and for greater tolerance of minority groups, notably homosexuals. Foucault himself was gay.

Along with fellow structuralist Claude Lévi-Strauss, Foucault rejected the view that human knowledge of the universe was based on the observation of the external world, saying that man was essentially a thinking animal who lived in a world that was intelligible to him only because he imposes his own order upon his experiences.

Social control

The relationship between human beings, said Foucault, could best be defined as a constant struggle for power. Right, wrong, truth and falsehood, he postulated, were all illusory, and were simply the creations of language and the will to dominate. He concluded there were no such things as benevolence and charity; rather, men built hospitals and set up schools and prisons not to cure, educate or reform but to control and subjugate others.

Looking to history for examples to prove his point, Foucault averred that the Enlightenment was not enlightened at all; its rationalism was a pretence, simply a mask to hide its social malevolence. In the 18th century, he continued, the term 'madness' was employed to categorize and stigmatize not just the mentally ill but the poor, the sick, the homeless and, indeed, anyone who looked like they were trying to upset the status quo. Similarly, Freud, with his invention of psychoanalysis, had given the establishment an even more powerful weapon. Controlling the mind, Foucault said, was a far more effective means of social control than punishing the body.

Categorization and objectification

Modern society, Foucault postulated, has found ways of classifying people – 'objectivism' was the name he gave to the process. The modes of division were 'dividing practices', 'scientific classification' and 'subjectification'. Dividing practices, said Foucault, objectified people by distinguishing and separating them from their fellows. Scientific classification means exactly what it says, but specification is slightly more complex. In Foucault's dark, pessimistic world, it refers to the way in which people actually consider themselves as subjects. It led people to form power relationships with authority figures as they tried to understand themselves better.

There were some grounds for optimism. Philosophy, said Foucault, could use his methods to expose the power structures that were intended to control us and help in the creation of new social structures

ABOVE: **Foucault believed that knowledge and power interact to produce the human self. His influence extended beyond philosophy to the rest of the humanities and the social sciences.**

Noam Chomsky

1928–

Noam Chomsky is one of the best-known thinkers of our time, and his work on the grammar of language has been pivotal in driving forward the study of linguistics. His radical political views have won him an international reputation as a pundit and controversialist.

Philosopher and radical

BELOW: **Chomsky believes that, as 'the vehicle of thought', language is uniquely positioned to reveal the nature and essence of the human mind.**

Educated at the University of Pennsylvania and at Harvard, Chomsky joined the Massachusetts Institute of Technology in 1955 and has taught there ever since. Long regarded as the most distinguished figure in American linguistics, he is also noted for his championship of radical political causes and views. Some of his views have been controversial, but even his sternest critics would not dispute the differences he has brought to intellectual life.

Revolutionizing linguistics

Chomsky's pioneering work in linguistics revolutionized the scientific study of language. It, he said, 'is the vehicle of thought' and so is uniquely placed to light up the essence of the human mind. He took as his starting point the rationalist philosophical viewpoint that, far from being a clean slate to be written on by experience as the empiricists had predicated, the mind possesses innate rational knowledge of its own. Nor were people free agents in the way existentialist thinkers presumed.

It was Chomsky's contention that all languages shared a fundamental universal grammar, which, he said, was hardwired into the human brain; it was not something that needed to be taught or learned. From this assumption, he went on to argue that countless syntactic combinations could be generated by the application of a complex set of rules.

A new grammar

Chomsky called what he was postulating 'transformational grammar'. According to him, every sentence obeys two sets of grammatical rules: the particular rules – the 'surface structures' – that apply to the particular language being spoken or written; and the rules imposed on language by what Chomsky termed the 'deep structures' within the human brain.

He went on to formulate 'transitional rules', by which a sentence with a given grammatical structure could be turned into one with a different structure while retaining the same meaning. The next step was to perfect what became known as the 'Chomsky hierarchy', in which formal grammar was divided into classes or groups of increasing expressive power.

Transitional linguistics

'Transitional linguistics', as Chomsky's new approach was dubbed, soon proved influential, particularly in psycholinguistics and the study of the acquisition of language by young children. Child psychologists had frequently observed that children aged around two and three seemed to develop grammatical ability far in advance of their limited language skills. Chomsky believed that the phenomenon conclusively proved his argument by showing that grammatical rules did not have to be learned. They are something innate within the mind, and it is early exposure to language that triggers them into action.

The consequences went far beyond the boundaries of linguistics. Thoughts, Chomsky postulated, are not simply conditioned responses to various stimuli, as early behavioural psychologists had believed; rather, all of us are endowed with innate properties that determine what we are like, what we can know and what we will tolerate insofar as the society in which we live is concerned.

BIOGRAPHY

Name Noam Chomsky

Born 1928

Place Philadelphia

Nationality American

Key facts The intellectual giant of our time and the author of more than 80 books and countless essays and articles, Chomsky is a true polymath, his work encompassing linguistics, politics and aspects of philosophy.

KEY WORKS

- *Syntactic Structures*
- *Aspects of the Theory of Syntax*
- *Language and Mind*
- *Knowledge of Language*

Bernard Williams

1929–2003

The outstanding moral philosopher of his generation, Williams effortlessly spanned the gamut of philosophy in his thinking. He investigated political theory, metaphysics and epistemology as well as probing deep into the nature of self and truth itself.

BIOGRAPHY

Name Bernard Williams

Born 1929

Place Westcliffe-on-Sea

Nationality British

Key facts Described as 'an analytical philosopher with the soul of a humanist', Williams, the most brilliant and important British moral philosopher of his time, singlehandedly revived the subject after years of decline.

Died 2003

KEY WORKS

• *Morality: An Introduction to Ethics*

• *Moral Luck*

• *Ethics and the Limits of Philosophy*

Coming to terms with life

Educated at Oxford, Williams was regarded as one of the most brilliant scholars of his day, rising to the top of the academic tree as Provost of King's College, Cambridge, and then, after a stint in the USA teaching philosophy at Berkeley, Professor of Moral Philosophy at Oxford. In his work he trenchantly criticized the moral thinking of the utilitarians and of Immanuel Kant and started the current philosophical debate on the notions of equality, personal identity and the self. Williams held that it was the duty of philosophers to come to terms with the complexities of human life, helping people to a greater sense of self-awareness and self-understanding.

For this reason Williams had little time for many of his predecessors, believing that much of the philosophy of the past constituted a flight from reality, ignoring what the world was actually like and the problems that really concern humankind. Taking refuge in a cloud-cuckoo-land of often incomprehensible postulations and arid speculations was something he found completely unacceptable. 'Writing about moral philosophy should be a hazardous business,' Williams wrote, but most thinkers, he said, ducked the issue. They were afraid of revealing 'the inadequacy of one's perceptions' and of 'misleading people about matters of importance'. The result, he concluded, was that they ended up 'refusing to write about anything of importance at all'.

How we should live

Williams was certainly no respecter of persons or reputations – he dismissed Aristotle tersely as 'boring' – but it was the ethical dogma of the utilitarians and of Immanuel Kant that he disliked the most, savagely criticizing utilitarianism on a number of grounds but particularly for its view that morality lay in seeking the greatest good for the greatest number. This, said Williams, was simply not so; the utilitarians totally

failed to engage with the real moral problems confronting philosophy, stripping human life of everything that made it worthwhile through their failure to take account of the importance of individual integrity, the projects central to a person's life and the special obligations and loyalty owed to family and friends. It was a powerful and extremely influential indictment.

Individuality and humanity

As for Kant, Williams especially disliked and disagreed with his reliance on the 'categorical imperative' in his efforts to define moral behaviour. Morality, he argued, did not require people to act selflessly. Nor should they be forced to take an impartial view of the world. Individual values, commitments and desires, Williams continued, do make a difference to the way we see the world and how we act in it. This was exactly how it should be, since, if we relinquish our individuality, we lose our humanity.

Above all else, Williams urged people to 'find your deepest impulse and follow that'. It is what he termed 'inner necessity' that drives us on to do what we do. Rather than asking Kant's question 'What is my duty?' philosophy should be asking how we should live.

ABOVE: **Williams believed that it was impossible to codify ethics into convenient moral theories. He argued that, in terms of the way people actually live, such a codification was not only unhelpful but impractical.**

Jacques Derrida

1930–2004

The founding father of deconstruction in philosophy, Jacques Derrida became one of the most celebrated – and, at the same time, controversial and difficult to follow – thinkers of the later part of the 20th century.

BIOGRAPHY

Name Jacques Derrida

Born 1930

Place El-Biar, Algeria

Nationality French

Key facts One of modern philosophy's great iconoclasts, Derrida was unique. Deconstruction, the philosophical system he invented as a reaction to the then voguish structuralist approach to language, was unlike anything that had gone before.

Died 2004

KEY WORKS

• *Of Grammatology*

• *Speech and Phenomena*

• *Writing and Difference*

Deconstruction

Derrida studied philosophy in Paris, where he was swept up in the great philosophical boom that transformed French thinking in the late 1960s. Young and charismatic, he soon built up a following, particularly in the USA, where he taught at John Hopkins University, Yale and the University of California. His thinking, however, made him as many enemies as it won him supporters, and it is still considered extremely controversial.

Derrida's system of deconstruction asserted that there was no such thing as truthfulness, fixed conceptual order or abstract meaning. Writing was contradictory and confusing, as it was unable to overcome the inherent contradictions of language itself. Given these premises, it is perhaps less than surprising that Derrida himself found deconstruction problematic to define precisely – indeed, he put forward several definitions during his career. Asked in an interview in 1998 to try yet again, he replied simply: 'It is impossible to respond. I can only do something that will leave me unsatisfied.'

Meaning and self

Meaning, said Derrida, was something that could be achieved or interpreted only from specific individual situations. Traditional signs were irrelevant, since they always signified things other than those that might be supposed. In other words, any sign can mean one thing at one particular time but another thing at another. Signs can never claim to be objective, nor is there any authority that can be invoked to support their interpretation.

Derrida was to go further. The idea of 'self' was nothing more than a linguistic construction: 'There is no subject who is agent, author and master of language.' The inescapable conclusion was that we are not rational, autonomous beings in charge of our language, meaning and – ultimately – thought.

A cult philosophy

Nevertheless, deconstruction, at least for a time, won a massive cult following among the Western intellectual elite. From its roots in linguistics it spread its tentacles to embrace the whole of the arts and the social sciences, including political science, anthropology and even literature and architecture. Literary critics deconstructed texts into isolated phrases to find hidden meanings. Radical supporters of gay rights, feminism and third-world causes used it to expose, so they claimed, the prejudices and prejudices of such 'dead white male' icons of Western culture as Plato, Aristotle and Shakespeare. Architects abandoned traditional symmetry in favour of zigzagging, sometimes disquieting, spaces. Even the actor, screenwriter and film-maker Woody Allen got in on the act. For one of his best-known movies, he chose the title *Deconstructing Harry*. It suggested, Allen said, that his film's protagonist could best be understood by tracking down and analysing his neurotic contradictions.

Popular as deconstruction became, it attracted as many critics as defenders. Derrida did not help his cause with his opaque explanations. One he produced in 1993, for instance, began: 'Deconstruction, if there is such a thing, takes place as the experience of the impossible.' It is little wonder that the *Economist* magazine stated that 'the trouble with reading Mr Derrida is that there is too much perspiration for too little inspiration'.

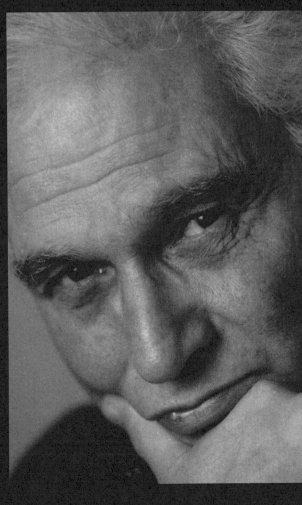

RIGHT: **Derrida opposed the structural view of language, arguing instead that, if it was to mean anything, language must be limited to expression, because only the latter conveyed sense.**

Robert Nozick

1938–2002

A one-time political radical who later turned libertarian neo-conservative, Nozick became the idol of the American right through his championship of individual rights and his call for the power of the state to be curtailed.

BIOGRAPHY

Name Robert Nozick

Born 1938

Place Brooklyn

Nationality American

Key facts Nozick won fame early. *Anarchy, State and Utopia*, his first book, published when he was only 36, became the philosophical bible of the American right.

Died 2002

KEY WORKS

• *Anarchy, State and Utopia*

Championing the individual

Like John Rawls, his Harvard colleague, Nozick opposed utilitarianism for its collectivism, instead favouring Kant's emphasis on individual rights instead. From there, the two men differed. Rawls said that the best form of society was social democracy, while Nozick emerged as the champion of full-blooded libertarianism. He argued that all individuals were what he termed 'self-owners'. Consequently, all individual rights were property rights, which no state had the power to override.

'Entitlement justice' and the free market

Nozick held that the state's role was limited to protecting its citizens from violence, theft and breach of contract. No one, he argued, who had legitimately acquired what he called 'holdings' could be put under any obligation to give them away. This was, he said 'entitlement justice'. For Nozick, state welfare was nothing more than institutionalized theft and any type of progressive taxation a form of forced labour. As for socio-economic development it was, he said, driven by the invisible hand of the free market, which was beyond anyone's power to control.

RIGHT: **Nozick was an advocate of extreme libertarianism, arguing that state welfare was nothing less than institutionalized theft and progressive taxation.**

Saul Kripke

1940–

Among the world's foremost living philosophers, Kripke established his international reputation through his groundbreaking work on modal logic, the philosophy of language, the nature of truth and the vexed question of being.

Modal logic

Kripke was a teenage prodigy, publishing his first thoughts on logic at the age of 19 and being elected a Fellow of Harvard while still a sophomore. Later, he became a professor at Rockefeller University and then at Princeton, where he taught until his retirement. So-called Kripke semantics, Kripke frames and Kripke models are all essential tools in modal logic – the logic of notions such as necessity and possibility – as it is practised today.

Language and truth

Kripke also pioneered a revolutionary new approach to language and metaphysics. He proposed replacing descriptivism – the idea that a name is applied to an object because of that name's association with a description of that object – with a new theory, which he called 'direct reference'. It stipulated that any name is simply a tag or label attached to its recipient.

Kripke then went on to propose a new theory of truth based on the idea that it was possible to create sentences that contained their own 'truth predicate', that is, a sentence with a construction that does not give rise to a paradox.

LEFT: **Kripke's revolutionary approach to modal logic and the truth theory helped establish him as a leading modern philosopher.**

BIOGRAPHY

Name Saul Kripe

Born 1940

Place Bay Shore, Long Island

Nationality American

Key facts Voted one of the top ten philosophers of the past 200 years by his peers, Kripke's influence on thinking has been immense, particularly in the fields of logic and linguistics.

KEY WORKS

- *Semantic Considerations on Modal Logic*
- *Naming and Necessity*

Glossary

ABSOLUTE An all-embracing principle, which some philosophers – notably Baruch Spinoza and Georg Wilhelm Friedrich Hegel – say is the source of all reality. Others have identified it with God.

AESTHETICS The branch of philosophy dealing with the nature and expression of beauty.

ANALYSIS Seeking a deeper understanding of a proposition by taking it to pieces. Whether an analytical statement is true or not can be established only by close analysis of the statement itself. The opposite is synthesis, which means seeking the same understanding by putting the pieces together. The validity of a synthetic statement can be determined only by setting it against known facts outside of itself.

ANALYTIC PHILOSOPHY Originally concerned with the analysis of language, it clarifies concepts, statements, arguments and theories by using logic to take them apart.

ANALYTICAL STATEMENT See **ANALYSIS**.

ANTINOMY Reaching contradictory conclusions from equally valid premises.

A POSTERIORI See **A PRIORI**.

A PRIORI Something that is known to be true or false before it is experienced. It is the opposite of a posteriori, which is something whose validity can be tested only through experience.

CATEGORIES The most basic groups into which things can be divided.

CAUSALITY The relationship between two things when the first is seen as causing the second.

COSMOLOGY The study of the universe or cosmos.

DEDUCTION A form of argument in which the conclusion logically follows from the initial premises, the general leading to the particular. The opposite – that is, reasoning from the particular to the general – is termed induction. Because it does not necessarily produce true results, some philosophers (notably David Hume and Karl Popper) have questioned whether it should be classed as a genuinely logical process or as a psychological one.

DETERMINISM The belief that any event is the inevitable outcome of specific preceding causes. The opposite belief, which holds that all human beings are free to determine their own actions, is free will.

DIALECTIC A philosophical method originated by Georg Wilhelm Friedrich Hegel and Karl Marx, in which apparent contradictions between two statements are reconciled by devising a synthesis containing elements of the two.

DUALISM The belief that reality consists of two basic elements, the one fundamentally different from the other. Its most celebrated advocate was René Descartes, who argued that all human beings possessed bodies and minds that were radically dissimilar.

ÉLAN VITAL Term coined by French philosopher Henri Bergson to describe the life force which he believed was the driving force behind the evolutionary process. Possessing it also distinguished the living from the non-living.

EMPIRICISM The notion that it is only possible to determine whether anything is true or not through actual experience.

EPISTEMOLOGY The branch of philosophy that concerns itself with the nature of knowledge – with what we know and how we know it – so establishing what limits, if any, there are to human understanding.

ESSENCE The qualities that make something what it is rather than anything else. It does not necessarily imply existence.

ETHICS The philosophical examination of human values, tackling such basic issues as how we should live, what is good and bad, right and wrong and other similar moral concepts.

EXISTENTIALISM A relatively modern philosophical movement that starts from the assumption that all people possess complete freedom of choice and are therefore personally responsible for what they make of themselves in life.

FREE WILL See **DETERMINISM**.

IDEALISM The view, held by such philosophers as Immannuel Kant and Georg Wilhelm Friedrich Hegel, that the world does not exist independently of the human mind and so reality is basically non-material. Its opposite is materialism, which says that only material things actually exist.

INDUCTION See **DEDUCTION**.

INTUITION A way of knowing that does not employ reasoning, instead depending on innate insight or perception.

LIBERTARIANISM A political philosophy whose advocates press for the greatest possible degree of freedom for individuals and the consequent minimization of state interference in individual life.

LOGIC The branch of philosophy concerned with rational argument, focusing on the structure of propositions and the principles of deductive reasoning.

LOGICAL POSITIVISM The belief that all philosophy must be based on observation and testing and that any proposition that cannot be verified, by definition, must be false.

MATERIALISM See **IDEALISM**.

METAPHYSICS The branch of philosophy concerned with what are termed 'first principles'. As well as enquiring into questions such as knowledge and being, it examines the ultimate nature of everything in existence.

MONISM The belief that reality is one unified whole and that everything in existence therefore is part of a single concept or system. Monism is the opposite of dualism.

NATURALISM The belief that reality can be understood without reference to anything outside or beyond the natural world.

NOMINALISM The belief that universals are unreal and non-existent. Rather, they are simply words and names for given phenomena.

ONTOLOGY The branch of philosophy that deals with the nature of being. It inquires into what actually exists, rather than examining the nature of our knowledge of it, as epistemology.

PHENOMENOLOGY A philosophical view pioneered by German philosopher Edmund Husserl, which holds that reality is relative and subjective and that objects have no independent existence.

POSITIVISM The belief that knowledge is limited to what can be verified by observation and understood through the use of scientific principles.

PRAGMATISM A development of empiricism, pragmatism interprets truth in terms of its practical effects. The American philosopher William James used this principal to try to measure 'truth' in terms of the usefulness of a particular belief or judgement to an individual's life.

RATIONALISM The view that reason is the fundamental source of all knowledge and that the only valid way of gaining knowledge of the world is by exercising it. Famous rationalist philosophers include René Descartes, Baruch Spinoza and Gottfried Leibniz.

REALISM The belief that universals have an independent existence outside the mind and that the essence of all things exists objectively in nature.

RELATIVISM The theory that there are no objective standards that can be applied to knowledge, truth and moral principles. If these are influenced by anything at all, this is by their historical or cultural context.

SCEPTICISM The belief that it is impossible to know anything for certain. Sceptics hold that since absolute knowledge is unattainable, doubt is therefore central to human knowledge and experience.

SCHOLASTICISM The philosophical methods employed in medieval European thinking between the 12th and the 14th centuries, the aim being to reconcile Christian thought with the teachings of Aristotle.

SOLIPSISM The belief that only the self can be said to exist.

SOPHIST A person whose aim in any philosophical dispute is simply to win the argument rather than to establish the truth.

STOICISM A school of philosophy that originated in Greece around 308 BC, which held that human happiness could be achieved only by accepting good and bad fortune with equanimity.

SYLLOGISM A method of reasoning in which a conclusion is drawn from two premises.

SYNTHESIS See **ANALYSIS**.

SYNTHETIC STATEMENT See **ANALYSIS**.

TELEOLOGY The study of ends or goals, which starts by assuming that there is a purpose to life and the universe and that, from this, it follows that there is also an overall blueprint that makes all development meaningful.

UNIVERSAL A property shared by all individual members of a specific class or a concept that can be applied to all the members of a group.

UTILITARIANISM An ethical theory devised by British philosopher Jeremy Bentham and later elaborated by John Stuart Mill, which holds that society should aim for the happiness of the greatest number and that 'good' should be defined in terms of pleasure and the absence of pain.

Index